CW00972537

12

2

18

VIEW OF
# DEVON

# VIEW OF
# DEVON

Described and photographed by
ROY J. WESTLAKE

ROBERT HALE · LONDON

© *Roy J. Westlake 1977*
*First published in Great Britain 1977*

ISBN 0 7091 6196 4

Robert Hale Limited
Clerkenwell House
Clerkenwell Green
London EC1

Photoset, printed and bound
in Great Britain by
REDWOOD BURN LTD.,
Trowbridge and Esher

*(Frontispiece) Statue of Sir Francis Drake on Plymouth Hoe.*

TO JEAN,
SALLY,
AND KEITH

# CONTENTS

|  |  |  |
|---|---|---|
|  | *Acknowledgements* | 10 |
|  | *Introduction* | 15 |
| 1 | Plymouth | 19 |
| 2 | The South Hams | 47 |
| 3 | Dartmoor | 77 |
| 4 | Torbay | 109 |
| 5 | Exeter (and Exe to Teign) | 133 |
| 6 | East Devon | 161 |
| 7 | North Devon | 189 |
|  | *End Piece* | 217 |
|  | *Index* | 219 |

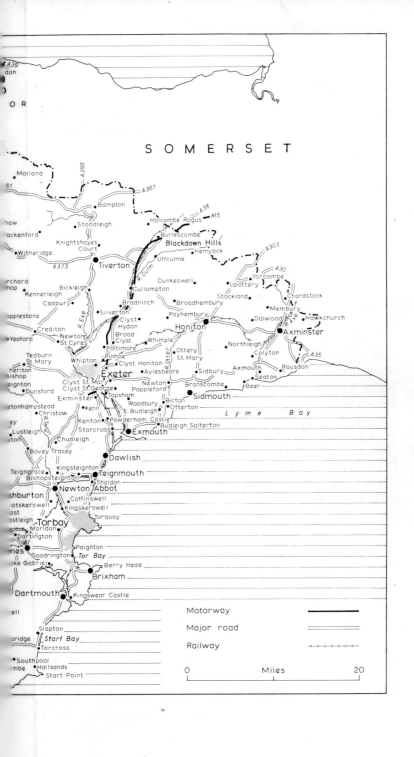

SOMERSET

A39
don

OR

Molland
61
aw
ackenford
Witheridge
rchard
hop
Kennerleigh
opplestone
Yeoford
Tedburn
St Mary
heriton
Bishop
eignton
Dunsford
etonhampstead
Christow
ey
Lustleigh
ton
shburton
otskerswell
ast
astleigh
nes
oke Gabriel
Dartmouth
ell
oridge
mbe

A396
Bampton
Stoodleigh
Knightshayes
Court
Tiverton
A373
Bickleigh
Cadbury
Crediton
Newton
St Cyres
Whipton
Bradninch
Silverton
Clyst
Hydon
Broad
Clyst
Poltimore
Pinhoe
Exeter
Clyst St Mary
Clyst St George
Exminster
Topsham
Kenn
E. Budleigh
Kenton
Powderham Castle
Starcross
Chudleigh
Bovey Tracey
Teigngrace
Bishopsteignton
Kingsteignton
Shaldon
Newton Abbot
Coffinswell
Kingskerswell
Torquay
Torbay
Marldon
Dartington
Goodrington
Paignton
Tor Bay
Berry Head
Brixham
Kingswear Castle

Holcombe Rogus
A38
M5
Burlescombe
Blackdown Hills
Uffculme
Hemyock
R.Culm
Cullompton
Dunkeswell
Broadhembury
Payhembury
Honiton
Whimple
Clyst Honiton
Aylesbeare
Ottery
St. Mary
Sidbury
Newton
Poppleford
Branscombe
Woodbury
Bicton
Otterton
Budleigh Salterton
Exmouth
Dawlish
Teignmouth

A303
A30
Upottery
Yarcombe
Stockland
Chardstock
Membury
Dalwood
Hawkchurch
Axminster
Northleigh
Colyton
A35
Axmouth
Rousdon
Seaton
Beer
Sidmouth

Lyme Bay

Slapton
Start Bay
Torcross
Southpool
Hallsands
Start Point

| Motorway | |
| Major road | |
| Railway | |

0          Miles          20

# ACKNOWLEDGEMENTS

I gratefully acknowledge assistance from a number of people and sources. Facts were supplied by Brian Brady, the County Press and Publicity Officer, also by Mike Weaver of the West Country Tourist Board and by the Dartmoor National Parks Office – and others – but interpretation and comments are entirely my own. Mines of information were C.W. Bracken's *History of Plymouth*, W.G. Hoskins' *Devon*, and W. Crossing's *Guide to Dartmoor*, all of which are standard works. Also numerous town guides, leaflets and ancient publications collected in my travels, or consulted in Plymouth's excellent Reference Library.

# ILLUSTRATIONS

| | |
|---|---|
| Map of Devon | 8—9 |
| The Barbican area of Plymouth | 18 |
| The replica of the *Golden Hind* | 22 |
| A re-enactment of the departure of the Pilgrim Fathers | 24 |
| The *Mayflower* Memorial | 25 |
| Plymouth Sound | 27 |
| Service display at The Hoe | 29 |
| The *Penn Ar Bed* leaving Millbay Docks | 32 |
| Plymouth's city centre after the Second World War | 34 |
| Charles Church | 35 |
| Multi-storey car park in Plymouth | 35 |
| Modern building in Plymouth | 36 |
| Drake Circus shopping complex, Plymouth | 37 |
| Plymouth's 'Grand Design' from the roof of the Civic Centre | 40—41 |
| View from the roof of the Civic Centre, Plymouth | 43 |
| Saltram House, Plympton | 44 |
| The River Plym at Plymbridge | 45 |
| The Yealm estuary | 46 |
| The beach at Mothecombe | 50 |
| Modbury | 53 |
| The tidal road between Bigbury and Aveton Gifford | 54 |
| Bigbury and Burgh Island | 55 |
| The coastline between Bolt Head and Salcombe | 57 |
| Mill Bay beach and Salcombe | 58 |
| The pontoon landing stage at Salcombe | 59 |
| Kingsbridge Creek | 61 |
| The coastline between Start Point and Strete | 62 |

| | |
|---|---|
| Slapton Sands from Torcross | 64 |
| Slapton Ley nature reserve | 65 |
| The Obelisk at Slapton | 66 |
| Blackpool Sands | 68 |
| The Tradesmen's Arms at Stokenham | 69 |
| The entrance to Dartmouth Harbour | 70 |
| The Inner Harbour at Dartmouth | 72–73 |
| Buckland Abbey | 76 |
| Lee Moor china clay pit on Dartmoor | 78 |
| Burrator Lake, with Sheeps Tor | 79 |
| Sheeps Tor from Ringmoor Down | 81 |
| Plymouth leat at Roborough Down | 83 |
| Devonport leat, near Nun's Cross | 84 |
| Princetown Prison | 86 |
| Meavy village | 87 |
| Vixen Tor, Dartmoor | 88 |
| Tavistock | 91 |
| The remains of Wheal Betsy pump house at Blackdown | 92 |
| Postbridge, spanning the East Dart River | 93 |
| Stone circles at Grimspound | 94 |
| Childe's Tomb Cross, at Fox Tor | 95 |
| The clock at Buckland-in-the-Moor church | 98 |
| The village green at North Bovey | 99 |
| The view from Haytor | 100 |
| Haytor Tramway | 101 |
| Bowerman's Nose, near Manaton | 103 |
| Dartmoor ponies on Roborough Common | 107 |
| Cockington Court | 108 |
| The harbour at Paignton | 111 |
| Goodrington beach, Paignton | 112 |
| Paignton beach and pier | 113 |
| The harbour and sea-front gardens at Torquay, seen from the Rock Walk | 114 |
| Thatcher Rock, near Torquay | 115 |
| Oldway House, Paignton | 117 |
| Locomotive of the Dart Valley Railway on the line between Paignton and Kingswear | 118 |
| Abbey Sands, Torquay | 120–121 |

The Torbay Aircraft Museum                                    123
Brixham Harbour                                               124
The statue of William of Orange on the quayside at
    Brixham                               125
The Butter Walk at Totnes                                    127
The East Gate straddling the High Street in Totnes           129
Dartington Hall, near Totnes                                 131
Exeter's Guildhall                                           132
The Norman gate tower of Rougemont Castle                    135
The Ship Inn, Exeter                                         136
Mol's Coffee House, Exeter                                   137
The Exeter Canal                                             139
The steam tug *St Canute* at I.S.C.A. Maritime Museum,
    Exeter                               140
The High Street, Exeter                                      143
Pedestrian precinct in Exeter                                144
Stepcote Hill, with St Mary Steps, Exeter                    145
St Mary Steps Church, Exeter                                 146
The West Front of Exeter Cathedral                           148
The nave of Exeter Cathedral                                 150
Close-up of the nave roof, Exeter Cathedral                  151
Astronomical clock in Exeter Cathedral                       152
Wood carving on underside of seat in Exeter Cathedral        153
The sea front at Dawlish                                     155
The railway line between Dawlish Warren and
    Teignmouth                           156
The beach at Teignmouth                                      158
Houses at Topsham                                            160
A cottage *orné* near Exmouth                                163
Orcombe Point, Exmouth                                       165
Hayes Barton, near East Budleigh, Raleigh's birthplace       166
Carved bench ends at East Budleigh Church                    168
The beach at Budleigh Salterton                              171
The beach at Sidmouth in winter                              172
A street in Sidmouth                                         173
The beach at Branscombe Mouth                                175
Open-top trams near Seaton                                   176
Pleasure craft at Axmouth                                    179

| | |
|---|---|
| Otterton village | 180 |
| Beer | 181 |
| The cliffs at Ladram Bay | 182 |
| The *Tivertonian* on the Tiverton Canal | 184 |
| The towpath along the Tiverton Canal | 185 |
| Swans on the Tiverton Canal | 186 |
| The view from Great Torrington | 188 |
| The coast at Hartland Quay | 191 |
| Clovelly Harbour | 192 |
| Cobbled steps in Clovelly | 193 |
| Bideford Quay | 195 |
| Statue of Charles Kingsley on Bideford Quay | 196 |
| Barnstaple's shopping centre | 199 |
| Lynmouth | 200–201 |
| The Tome Stone at Barnstaple | 203 |
| Saunton Sands | 205 |
| Ilfracombe Harbour | 207 |
| Chambercombe Manor | 208 |
| Molland church | 211 |
| Sheep on a North Devon by-way | 213 |
| Malmsmead and Badgworthy Water | 214 |
| Woody Bay | 215 |
| Hay-making on a North Devon farm | 216 |

# INTRODUCTION

I WELL REMEMBER when about five or six years old travelling down from London and being collected from Ivybridge Station by pony and trap. My father was exiled in London, but 'the family' had a large farm in the area and this was reached through narrow twisting Devon lanes whose hedges were ablaze with primroses.

I can recall the rich, earthy smell of the shippen; the steamy atmosphere as the cows were hand-milked on a wet day, and the *swish-swish* of milk into a special pail which was always kept polished until you could see your face in it. Later, sneaking into the cool, underground dairy where butter was being made, I would beg odd pieces from the butter-pat to spread on bread freshly baked in the kitchen. There was a rambling orchard to explore with apples and pears enough to delight any small boy and to cause the most exquisite of stomach aches.

That was all more than forty years ago. The station buildings and goods yard still exist although no passenger has alighted there for many years. Inter-City trains thunder over the long viaduct which spans the River Erme and flash past the overgrown station as they gather speed on the long downhill gradient over Hemerdon Bank and thence on to the outskirts of Plymouth.

The farmhouse, shippen and other farm buildings are still there today, mellowed by age, and sadly reduced in size through the eyes of an adult. What I did not realize all those years ago was that the sole water supply was from a spring some distance away, via a handpump which often ran dry in the summer and froze solid in the winter. (The sanitary arrangements were also distinctly primitive, but quite usual for a country house.)

Whilst I lay abed in the morning others were up at 5 a.m. light-ing the great coal range, or starting work in the fields – work which, in fine weather, continued until 10 or 11 at night. When it rained there were always the odd carpentry jobs to be done, such as repairing the massive cart used to carry turnips or cattle food to the fields – or polishing and trimming the many paraffin lamps. No one on a farm was ever idle, yet it was a satisfying life.

Now there is mains water, electricity, a fridge and colour tele-vision – but also a four-lane dual carriageway road cutting a wide swathe across the landscape a few hundred yards from the house. This decimates the fields so that it is no longer a working farm. Such is the price we pay for progress.

Heavy lorries grind up the slight incline carrying manufactured goods – colour television sets amongst others – from the light in-dustries around Plymouth, or farm produce from France imported on the Roscoff–Plymouth ferry.

Holidaymakers, in ever-increasing numbers, stream down the road from Exeter with their caravans and boats as the last gap is filled in the M5 motorway and the Midlands and North daily come ever closer.

In an overpopulated island such as ours it is inevitable that parts of Devon will suffer from one of its main industries – tourism. During the summer months the more popular parts of the coastal strip grow a mushroom crop of trailer caravans which joins the older established and more regimented ranks of the permanent holiday caravans. There is always a risk that overcrowding will destroy the very qualities that bring visitors to an area, but so far Devon appears to have survived the annual invasion remarkably well. The fact that visitors return year after year must prove that they in turn are well satisfied that the character of Devon is not changing too fast.

Away from the hustle and bustle of the north and south coastal strips the hinterland has a timeless quality. Primroses and bluebells still grow in haphazard profusion in the hedgerows of the steep-banked country lanes that wind like drunken snakes across the countryside. Many years ago the track from which a road grew took a ninety-degree turn to avoid someone's duckpond or hay-stack. No one has seen any necessity to straighten its course since

and we still follow the same tortuous route – perhaps with a muffled curse as we approach each blind bend – but isn't this reduced
pace really one of the attractions of the countryside?

For the loner, there is also solitude in the heart of Dartmoor
where the sound of a peewit and the wind rustling the stiff marsh
grass are one's only companions – or in the quiet of a country
church. One can also find solitude on many parts of the coast away
from popular beaches. The South West Peninsula Footpath – to
quote its full and rather pretentious title – gives formal recognition
to paths and tracks that have existed for many, many years and
have been enjoyed by generations of walkers. On a cliff with no
sound but the mewing of gulls wheeling above and the rumble of
waves pounding on the rocks far below one may enjoy a well-
earned rest after a muscle-aching climb up some of Devon's more
dramatic coastline. Long may these oases of calm continue to exist
in a restless, thrusting world.

I hope these photographs and words will convey some of the
character of this historic and colourful countryside. Few other
counties can rival the variety of scenery to be found in Devon,
from the lush meadows of the South Hams to the rolling hills of
Exmoor; from the red sandstone cliffs and Mediterranean-blue sea
of Torbay to the long sandy beaches of Saunton and Woolacombe
in the north. In between there is Dartmoor, a wilderness of jagged
tors and heather-covered hills. I have attempted – however inad-
equately – to capture something of all these aspects of a delightful
county.

The Barbican area, a polyglot mass of fishing boats with foreign-sounding names, a pleasure-boat marina and, in the foreground, the Kathleen and May, last of the North Devon trading schooners.

CHAPTER ONE

# PLYMOUTH

PLYMOUTH? "Ah yes, that's that naval place down at the bottom end of Devon. We passed through there on our way to Cornwall last year. Drake came from there, didn't he? – and the Pilgrim Fathers."

Fair comment on most visitors' mental picture of Plymouth? Well, perhaps not, but it is astonishing how few people outside the south-west fully appreciate Plymouth's background and place in history. The penalty, no doubt, for the poor road communications that have plagued the area for centuries. Plymouth has always looked seawards – at least until very recent times. The limestone promontory on which a huddle of fishermen's dwellings grew to a city of some 250,000 people is surrounded on three sides by water, so it is not remarkable that the sea should have played such an important part in its history. A surprisingly short recorded history, mark you, but a highly eventful one.

Daniel Defoe, that keen-eyed inveterate traveller, passed this way in the eighteenth century and commented:

Plymouth is indeed a Town of Consideration, and of great importance to the public. The situation of it [is] between two large inlets of the Sea, and in the bottom of a large bay, which is remarkable for the advantage of navigation. The Sound, or Bay, is compass'd on every side with hills, and the shore generally steep and rocky, tho' the anchorage is good, and it is pretty safe riding.

That would be equally true today; but what of the past? There are some traces of Stone Age man – but not many – and the Romans appear to have trod lightly on the area, using it rather as a transit camp on their way to and from Exeter when exploiting the Cornish tin mines.

Saxons conquered the Celtic tribes and stayed until they in turn were ousted by William the First, who rewarded his adventurous Norman knights with their estates. At the time of the Domesday Survey in 1086 it was a small hamlet of fishermen's cottages in the royal manor of Sudtone (later Sutton). Today, historians are grateful for the very detailed record of land, cattle, etc. contained in Domesday, but it is worth remembering that it was prepared primarily as an assessment of taxable possibilities and no doubt the population received the King's officials with less than enthusiasm. Their grumbles and protests over unreasonable assessments are contained in the Anglo-Saxon Chronicle and these strike a cord of sympathy today!

The waterside community grew steadily under the Normans and fell eventually into the hands of the Priors of Plympton, whose Augustinian monastery several miles away had been founded much earlier. By the early fourteenth century the name of Plymouth was in general use for the area covered by three manors – Sutton Prior, Sutton Valletort and Sutton Ralf – the first still controlled by the Priors, the other two by their respective lords of the manor. Prompted by a particularly disastrous raid by the French in 1403 and the obvious need for adequate defences, the people attempted to shake themselves free from these restrictive, if benevolent, patrons.

After a prolonged political struggle, in 1439 Plymouth was granted a Charter by Act of Parliament. It thus became the first truly incorporated borough in the country, for all others previously had been obtained by royal grant. Now with a population exceeding 7,000, a mayor, a corporation, the right to hold a market – and a harbour of importance to the King's Navy – Plymouth probably ranked as fourth city in the land. (It is not surprising that Plymouth's demotion to the status of a District Council in recent times should be resented in this proud city – but more of this later.)

Defence inevitably occupied the attention of the new corporation for a number of years. A small castle with four towers already existed – from which the present-day coat of arms derives

— but now new 'bulwarks' were built along the sea front, backed by cannon. The offshore island of St Nicholas (later renamed Drake's Island) was fortified and every able-bodied person was required to do a share of look-out duty. No doubt the 'watch' was not a popular chore, but these measures helped the town to grow without further harassment.

Elizabeth had always looked favourably on Devon, and Plymouth in particular. These were stirring times and when she came to power the stage was set for the 'Golden Age' of sea power; Hawkins, Gilbert, Raleigh and, of course, Drake were all waiting in the wings. What do we know of Drake, the greatest seafarer of them all? He was born at Tavistock, about eleven miles from Plymouth, in 1541 — the exact date is not known — and married Mary Newman at St Budeaux Church (now within the city) in 1569.

He learnt his seamanship from John Hawkins and learnt it well; he had an excellent memory and was a superb navigator. A man given to quick decisions and brusque actions, he could still plan methodically and with foresight when the situation demanded. Physically he was "low of stature, of strong limbs, broad breasted, round-headed, brown-haired, full bearded, his eyes round large and clear, well-favoured and of a cheerful countenance". Bluff and outspoken, at times arrogant and overbearing, he obtained loyalty from his men and was remarkably merciful in his treatment of prisoners. He could also be diplomatic when it suited his purpose — on one occasion he accepted a subsidiary role under Hawkins' overall command, at Elizabeth's insistence.

A smouldering 'undeclared' state of war had existed with Spain for many years and it was believed that Philip would eventually use the treasure shipped from Peru and Mexico to pay for the equipping of a fleet with which to attack England. Here was a case where the English 'legalized privateers', by attacking the Spanish treasure fleets, could serve their country's cause and at the same time further their own fortunes.

Royal patronage depended upon successful results and these daring captains with their superb seamanship served the Queen well — and the royal coffers benefited accordingly. Plymouth became a clearing house for prizes taken at sea and a new quay was built to handle the wealth flowing into the port.

*Of all the famous craft to depart from Plymouth's waters, this replica of the Golden Hind had the greatest benefit of press and television coverage. It shows the sheer smallness of Drake's original boat that encircled the world.*

In 1577, Drake set sail with five ships, ostensibly on a trading expedition to Alexandria. This innocuous trip developed – as perhaps Drake had always intended – into a circumnavigation of the globe. He took several Spanish prizes on his way and became the first Englishman to pass through the Magellan Strait and to explore the western coast of the American continent, returning round the Cape of Good Hope.

Of his original fleet only the *Pelican* – renamed the *Golden Hind* – survived, a ship smaller than most modern trawlers. She was laden down with treasure and leaking badly when in September 1580 Drake sailed triumphantly into Plymouth Sound – only to find the town smitten by plague, Elizabeth making peace overtures to Spain and his 'treasure hunting' a diplomatic embarrassment. Within months, in the cut and thrust of political intrigue, Philip landed troops in Ireland; this gave Elizabeth the excuse to acknowledge Drake and he sailed up channel to Deptford, to a hero's welcome.

Philip viewed Drake's prowess and seamanship with rather less enthusiasm and after numerous insults including the 'Singeing of the King's Beard' in Nombre de Dies Bay and Cadiz, the King succeeded in assembling an armada of 129 ships and 32,000 men to sail against England. It was sighted off the Lizard on 19 July 1588, sailing under favourable winds. Drake, as we all know, was playing bowls on Plymouth Hoe when the news reached him and he declined to hurry. Cynics – or perhaps realists – may say that he had ample time to finish his game whilst waiting for tide and wind to change sufficiently to clear the harbour. Most, I am sure, would prefer to regard this as a superb example of steady nerves and 'unflappability'. The story, incidentally, is almost certainly true for it was circulating in 1624, within living memory of the event. On one point we can be certain: his statue stands today close to the spot where the game would most likely have been played, with his eyes fixed firmly on the distant horizon.

The Armada was 'drummed up the Channel', thrown into confusion by fire ships, and finally scattered by gales. Only fifty-four ships straggled back to Spain. As the inscription on the Hoe Armada Memorial – erected 300 years later – says, "He blew with his winds and they were scattered", although it is not clear

*A re-enactment of the departure of the Pilgrim Fathers. In the background is the Island House in which they are reputed to have spent their last night. On the wall, a plaque quoting the names of all who sailed in the* Mayflower.

whether this gives the credit to Drake, or the deity – or both!

In its time Plymouth has welcomed home many famous ships and sailors, including Sir Francis Chichester after *his* circumnavigation of the world. As *Gypsy Moth III* entered the Sound on 28 May 1967 against a setting sun and attended by a flotilla of escorting craft, he received a tumultuous welcome from the crowds thronging the slopes of the Hoe.

However, perhaps the best-known ship of them all entered the harbour in the summer of 1620, to a quieter welcome, but all aboard the *Mayflower* were "kindly entertained and courteously used by divers friends there dwelling". This group of English Puritans had made two false starts on their voyage to America, setting sail first from Southampton, then putting into Dartmouth for

The Mayflower Memorial commemorates the sailing of the Pilgrim Fathers on 6 September 1620 after being "kindly entertained and courteously used by divers friends there dwelling".

repairs, before limping battered and dispirited into Plymouth.

Most of their troubles were caused by the *Speedwell* – their second ship – which was much smaller than the *Mayflower* (60 tons to the *Mayflower*'s 180 tons) and leaked badly. They decided to abandon her, and when the party finally left from the Barbican Causeway on 6 September all 102 men, women and children were crammed into the *Mayflower*. As 'amateur' sailors they showed remarkable skill and fortitude in tackling the vigours of an Atlantic voyage in the late autumn and making a landfall in New England.

When the Civil War broke out, Plymouth, almost alone in the West Country, declared for Parliament against the King. Perhaps because of its sea-going connections it was more outward looking than its neighbours. No doubt too this highly independent town resented King Charles' interference in the running of its domestic affairs. One particular quarrel had been over the appointment of a vicar for St Andrew's Church; the King had insisted on his nominee being accepted against the wishes of the townspeople. Their reply was to build another church – ingeniously named Charles Church – to which they could appoint a man of their own choice.

However, Charles Church would have to remain half-finished until the end of the siege three years later. During that time the people suffered attack, blockade and near-starvation. Plymouth's greatest danger was when Prince Maurice's army nearly overran the town in the winter of 1643. After initially taking a strategic hill, the Cavaliers were confused by a small band of defenders who attacked from the rear. They dropped back in disarray down the slopes of Lipson Hill and the retreat became a rout as they attempted to cross the tidal creek at the bottom. A monument in Freedom Fields Park commemorates their ignominious defeat!

Not surprisingly, when Charles II came to the throne at the Restoration he did not look kindly on the town that had defied his father. Traditional and constitutional rights were swept aside and many prominent citizens were thrown into jail.

Next the King appropriated land to the east of the Hoe upon which to build a citadel. Started in 1666 and completed about seven years later, this massive structure of granite and limestone – with perimeter walls covering more than a quarter of a mile – not only dominated the Sound, but also the town below. The point

*A view hardly to be equalled in Britain. Plymouth Sound seen from the ramparts of the ancient citadel, and right – on the grassy slopes of the Hoe – the unmistakable shape of Smeaton's Tower.*

was not lost on the populace that there were as many cannon overlooking the town as facing seawards!

The entrance was – and still is – an imposing gateway of Portland stone with elaborate carving and a niche in which once stood a statue of the King. Three cannon balls now fill the vacant space. In its heyday it mounted 165 guns spaced around the bastions and curtain walls, all of which were named.

The King paid several visits during its building, and on 17 July 1671, accompanied by his brother James and his son, the Duke of Monmouth, he landed at the Barbican steps. The citadel was far from complete so they stayed at the old fort – no doubt in some discomfort. The next day was spent inspecting the harbours of

Hamoaze and Cattewater in the "six frigates and seven pleasure boats that attended them".

It is recorded that the visit cost the town £219 1s. 8d., most of that sum being for a purse of gold to be presented to the King. Plymouth did not get good value for its money, for even this gesture of goodwill did nothing to appease him and in 1683 when many towns were forced to surrender their charters, Plymouth was treated with special ferocity. The hard-won charter was emasculated and the powers of the Corporation drastically reduced.

James II restored the town's privileges, but too late. When William of Orange landed at Brixham in November 1688, Plymouth was the first borough in the country to declare for him. As he was carried ashore by local fishermen he is recorded as having said in broken English: "Mine goot people, I mean you goot. I am come here for your goot, for all your goots." Perhaps not the greatest 'glad to be here' speech, with its overtones of ambiguity, but at least he was sincere.

Nor did he forget Plymouth when he later ascended the throne. For many years it had been realized that the broad shores of the Hamoaze presented a superb site for a dockyard; Raleigh had pointed out to Elizabeth that it was suitable "for a great design in a small space". Now under William III it was started. The first turf was cut at Point Froward, close to the waters that had sheltered his fleet after he had landed at Brixham.

This remarkable natural harbour within a harbour, landlocked and comparatively deep, is approached through a narrow channel some 500 yards wide at Devil's Point. The works proceeded apace and the area came to be known as Dock. Although only a few miles away from Plymouth, the two communities regarded themselves as separate entities, and before long, in the feverish activity of the Napoleonic Wars, the young upstart was outstripping the older town, first in population and then in importance.

This rivalry was exemplified in a squabble over water. Plymouth refused a request from Dock for a fresh-water supply and this resulted in the Dockers building another leat alongside the one that Drake had originally built to supply Plymouth. Then the Corporation decided, too late, that it had ample water for both! This none-too-friendly rivalry would not be finally patched up until the amalgamation in 1914 of the 'three towns', Plymouth, Dock (now called Devonport), and the 'buffer state' of Stone-house.

The Dockyard went from strength to strength. The original South Yard with its sail lofts, rigging and rope stores was extended. A North Yard was built in 1844 to cater for the advent of steam power. More basins and workshops were added, until by the middle of the eighteenth century this vast conglomeration became one of the most important dockyards in the world, and Plymouth's largest employer of labour.

Today it covers more than 320 acres and is still the city's biggest employer and a vital factor in Plymouth's economy. Records show that more than 255 ships and two floating docks have been built

*The Hoe forms an ideal venue for every kind of event, from service displays to fireworks. Some feel that such hallowed ground should be treated with more respect, but no doubt the ghosts of Drake and his illustrious colleagues enjoy the show.*

over the centuries, including several *Dreadnought* battleships, submarines and – largest of all – the 27,500 ton *Warspite* which was laid down in 1912. What the records do not stress is the vast amount of purely repair and maintenance work carried out on every conceivable type of ship – in fact, this has been the Dockyard's main function. In recent years, the Navy's aircraft carriers have been maintained here and much work carried out on guided missile frigates.

Fourteen miles off Plymouth Hoe lies the dangerous Eddystone Reef, mostly submerged and a constant danger to shipping. It was realized in the seventeenth century that some form of light was needed, but who would draw up the plans? Someone once defined an optimist as the designer of the first aeroplane and a pessimist as the designer of the first parachute. Perhaps lighthouse designers also need unbounded optimism; Henry Winstanley certainly did.

He was a merchant in London who, having lost two ships on this deadly reef, set about building a tower and light. He had so much confidence in his polygonal stone tower with its open galleries and weird projections that he expressed a wish to be in it "in the fiercest storm that ever blew". By coincidence, on 20 November 1703 he had his wish. That evening one of the fiercest storms ever to rage down the coast left a trail of destruction and sunken ships. In the morning the lighthouse, its designer and keepers were gone, and the rock was as bare as if a tower had never existed.

Next Rudyard built a tower – partly of wood – and this stood for nearly half a century, until it was destroyed by fire. John Smeaton, learning from his predecessor's mistakes, built the next lighthouse of granite outside and Portland stone for the interior. Shaped like the trunk of an oak tree with all the stone blocks interlocking in an ingenious fashion, its light shone out over the Channel for 123 years. In 1882 it was found that the sea had undermined the rock on which it stood and a much higher tower was built on an adjoining rock. Smeaton's Tower was dismantled stone by stone and the upper section re-erected on the Hoe, a landmark and popular viewpoint visited by thousands of people every year. They climb the narrow, twisting staircase – banging their heads against the low roof on the way – then up a series of wooden ladders to reach the open gallery at the top.

Plymouth's Sutton Harbour and Cattewater had been adequate in Elizabethan times for small fleets of shallow draught boats, but as ships grew larger the need for a deeper, more sheltered anchorage became obvious. This need was not to be completely met until 1841, when a 1,700-yard long breakwater was built across the Sound.

Plymouth now had its safe anchorage and full use of this was to be made in the years ahead. Before the Second World War about 600 liners a year used the harbour, including the *Normandie* in 1937, on her record-breaking Atlantic crossing. *Doidge's Western Counties Annual* for 1932 carries an advertisement for the French Line offering a weekly service to New York, plus ships to Santander, Corunna and the West Indies. Not to mention a number of cross-channel services.

Passengers were landed by the Great Western Railway's tenders, whisked through Customs and then boarded a special train waiting in Millbay Docks. Four hours later they – and the mail – could be in London whilst the liner continued up Channel at a more leisurely pace to dock at Southampton the next day.

With the expansion of air travel, mail and passengers could be carried even faster and the liner traffic declined. The Navy also wanted more room to manoeuvre its larger warships and the commercial port gradually stagnated. In recent times there has been a very welcome revival. Through the initiative of a French-owned company, Brittany Ferries (why not British, I wonder; Drake must be having a terrible time turning in his grave), there are roll-on, roll-off ferry services to Roscoff and St Malo. Despite its Russian-sounding name, Roscoff is near Morlaix in Brittany.

The ferry is one of the most important developments to hit Plymouth for many a long year. Huge articulated lorries with strange-looking continental plates trundle off the boats at a rate of 7,000 or so a year, like a latter-day invasion fleet. In season, they carry agricultural produce – from artichokes to cauliflowers – out of season, anything and everything to tickle the palates of lovers of fine food, or to ease the lot of the housewife.

British firms were slow at first to take advantage of this golden opportunity to bypass the more congested Channel ports, but in the past three years traffic has increased dramatically and this

*The roll-on, roll-off ferry service to France is one of the most important developments in recent years. Here the* Penn Ar Bed *leaves Millbay Docks en route to Roscoff in Brittany.*

outlet to the Continent now carries farm machinery, china clay, fish, meat, livestock, etc. The general public – on both sides of the Channel – has never had any doubts about the advantages; close on 140,000 passengers were carried in 1975, with a dramatic increase to 300,000 in 1976. In summer, the three ships are full of holiday-bound West Country registered cars, while the ladies of Brittany do their shopping in Plymouth's shops. During 'sale' times the stores – particularly those selling clothes – echo to strange French accents, bargains are struck with Gallic gestures, and the acrid smell of Gauloises pervades the air.

Back in 1939 Plymouth's city centre was an unplanned, rambling, friendly sort of place with narrow streets, blind corners and a tolerant mixture of cars, trams and pedestrians all cheek-by-jowl in the embryonic traffic jams. Union Street was the only truly straight thoroughfare – a roisterous haunt of Jack ashore, with more than thirty pubs, four cinemas and two music halls. The challenge was to start at Stonehouse, visit each pub in turn and still be capable of standing on reaching the railway bridge at the Plymouth end.

Hitler's bombs changed all that! In two terrible nights in March 1941 high explosive bombs tore the heart out of the city. What these did not flatten, incendiaries burnt. Shops, churches, theatres, cinemas and offices were indiscriminately reduced to blackened ruins. Further from the centre row upon row of houses overnight became heaps of rubble or burnt-out shells, blasted by bombs, land-mines and incendiaries. A thousand men, women and children died and nearly four thousand homes were destroyed. The destruction continued spasmodically until Plymouth had the doubtful distinction of being the worst blitzed city in the land at that time. There is still in existence a wartime map of Plymouth which looks like a devil's dartboard. Each black spot represents where at least one high explosive bomb fell; in places, particularly around the city centre and dockyard, it is almost impossible to separate the individual spots.

Even while bombs were still falling and long before the invasion fleets assembled in 1944 for 'D Day', plans were being made for the rebuilding of Plymouth. The City Engineer, James Paton Watson, was given the brief to design a new centre for Plymouth – a city of the future. He and Sir Patrick Abercrombie formulated the 'Plan for Plymouth' which attracted world-wide attention.

The plan envisaged the virtual clearance of all buildings from the centre and a fresh start with a blank sheet, using the contours to best advantage. A grid system of roads was to be built with tree-lined avenues and shopping precincts; a key road was to run from east to west. This was later to be named Royal Parade when in 1947 the King and Queen came to open the first stage of Plymouth's rebuilding.

Let's look at the outcome of the Plan, only slightly modified from the original concept. The best place from which to do this is the roof of the fourteen-storey Civic Centre. For a few pence one is whisked to the top by high-speed lift and there laid out below is the modern city, with the hills of Dartmoor away on the horizon.

Royal Parade, a wide dual carriageway — it would have been even wider if rising costs had not cut the original concept — is backed by the still gleaming Portland stone of the first stores and offices to be rebuilt — Dingle's, John Yeo's and Spooners (now Debenhams), and the Co-operative and Prudential Office building. Opposite is the Guildhall, once gutted, now rebuilt on two floors within the shell of the original building, and providing a magnificent conference-cum-concert hall.

Beyond again is St Andrew's Church. The morning after it was gutted during the war, a sign with the single word 'Resurgam' was erected above the north porch, the idea of a Plymouth school-teacher — Margaret Smith. Although it was to be many years before the building could be restored, open-air services were held in the ruin and the sign encouraged local people in the belief that

*Plymouth's city centre, soon after the end of the Second World War. Royal Parade is taking shape on the left, St Andrew's Cross roundabout is there in outline, but many of the buildings are gutted and roofless, including St Andrew's Church and the Guildhall.*

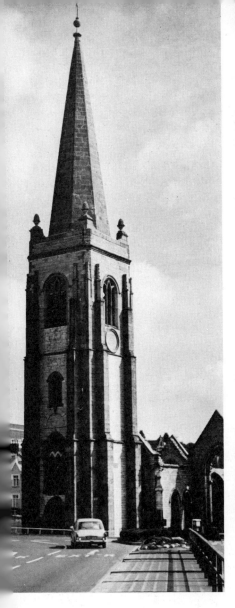

The city old and new. (Left) The graceful spire of Charles Church kept as a memorial to the civilian dead of the last war. (Right) Only a few yards away, the chunky staircase of a multi-storey car park.

Later buildings are stark, functional and striking. Who could fail to be impressed by this, but does it have character?

This small area certainly has a character of its own. Looking from the Drake Circus shopping complex towards St Andrew's Cross, past pleasant raised gardens and much-appreciated seats.

the city would rise again. Rebuilt now, it contains several of John Piper's bold stained-glass windows to add piquancy to the interior.

Behind the Guildhall and slightly right is the Barbican – a composite term for Sutton Harbour, together with all the quays and buildings of old Plymouth which adjoin the Cattewater. The masts of the *Kathleen and May* pierce the skyline above the warehouse roofs. She is the last of the North Devon topsail trading schooners and is now at a permanent berth where many a similar ship will have tied up in the past. Launched in 1900, she carried in her time cargoes of cement, potash, coal, clay and even gunpowder – in fact, any commercial cargo that would make a profit. Eventually she came to rest at Appledore, no longer economical to work and apparently destined to become a rotting hulk.

By good fortune, she was found by the newly formed Maritime Trust who took on the mammoth task of restoration. At Mashford's boatyard at Cremyll new masts were fitted, part of the bulwarks renewed, all rotten timber replaced and a new floor provided in the hold for a 'Sailing Ships' exhibition which is visited by thousands of holiday-makers every year. I had the double pleasure of photographing for the Maritime Trust the restoration work as it was carried out and her final dignified passage under tow, across the Sound, past Drake's Island, to her last permanent mooring.

The area round and about is packed with history – the old Customs House, the Island House where the Pilgrim Fathers are reputed to have stayed before sailing, the *Mayflower* Memorial commemorating their place of departure, the plaque remembering the sailing of the *Tory* in 1839 (a pioneer ship in the colonization of New Zealand), and, tucked away in cobbled New Street, the sixteenth-century 'Elisabethan House'. This is the essence of Plymouth's history, all within a space of a few hundred yards.

The fish quay – looking rather like an errant railway station – is still busy and a new marina close by provides moorings for hundreds of pleasure craft. Generally, the Corporation has rebuilt and restored around the Barbican area with taste and tact, but as always, there are the odd buildings which must have slipped through during a planners' tea break.

Let's return briefly to our vantage point at the top of the Civic Centre. Amidst the many large and palatial stores is the blue-domed roof of the Pannier Market. Inside is a fascinating hotch-potch of stalls, where you can rummage through 'antiques' or 'junk' (the definition depending on whether you are buyer or seller), buy 'non-packaged' foods brought in direct from the farm, or eat a hand-held pasty without embarrassment.

To our left Royal Parade merges into Union Street, the junction marked by the garish Drake Cinema. The railway bridge and embankment carrying the line from Millbay Docks have now gone leaving an ugly scar yet to be filled. Far beyond are the cranes and paraphernalia of the Dockyard, whilst just visible are the distant towers of the Tamar Bridge. An old 'across the border' joke has credited generations of Plymouthians with threatening to cut the chains of Torpoint Ferry and letting Cornwall float away, should 'Cousin Jack' become too upperty – particularly on Saturdays when Argyle is playing at home! Now the danger has been averted, for the Duchy is firmly anchored by the massive spans of the Tamar road bridge opened in 1961. Brunel was first with his unique railway suspension bridge in 1859, but that's another story.

Perhaps the best should always be left until last, and if we turn seawards the view is superb. A tree-lined lawn sweeps to the top of the limestone promontory that is the Hoe. The flat, tarmacadamed brow serves as a parade ground for service events, hard-standing for veteran car rallies, a grandstand for firework displays – or perhaps one of the finest places just to stand and look out to sea. Beyond, the Sound is alive with shipping of every conceivable shape and size, from canoes of the Adventure Centre on Drake's Island to the occasional aircraft carrier *en route* to the Dockyard.

In summer, the multicoloured sails of dinghies weave intricate patterns across the blue waters. An average of three class sailing championships is held here each year and with five slipways giving access to a large area of sheltered water it is not difficult to see why. Pleasure boats leave frequently for 'trips around the warships' (a

(Overleaf) *The heart of the city's 'Grand Design', seen from the roof of the Civic Centre. Royal Parade is on the left, with still gleaming Portland stone shop-fronts. To the right, the Guildhall and St Andrew's Church beyond.*

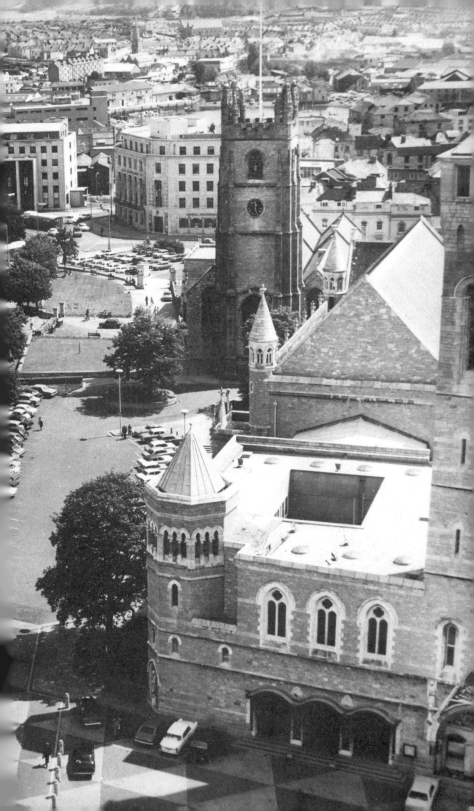

change at least from 'trips around the bay'), or travel further afield to Calstock on the River Tamar and Newton Ferrers on the Yealm estuary. The Millbrook Steamboat Company operate the trips from Phoenix Wharf on the Barbican in the 'Belles' – *Western Belle, Plymouth Belle*, etc. These 'steamers' have been a part of the Plymouth scene for many years and are a pleasant way of viewing the Hoe from seawards, or travelling up the rivers.

The occasional warship makes stately way through the lesser fry, whilst the comings and goings of the white-hulled Brittany Ferries as they cleave their way across the Sound add urgency to the scene.

The list of sailing events starting and finishing in the Sound reads like an international sailing calendar – Tall Ships, Round Britain, Fastnet, Transatlantic, etc., etc. Most are run under the auspices of the Royal Western Yacht Club.

For the past 500 years or so, the sea has been Plymouth's life-blood. Inland, communications were poor. Even in recent times the A38 – the longest lane in England, as many a holidaymaker will remember it – contributed nothing to the rapid movement of goods or people. Now all that has changed. With the completion of the M5 and a dual carriageway from Exeter onwards, factories on the outskirts of the city producing anything from colour television sets to oil filtration plant, from shoes to chewing gum, all have good outlets by land and sea. From the air, Plymouth's suburbs look like a casually thrown coil of rope, the whorls and loops of roads alternately enclosing factories, housing estates and precinct shopping centres.

Under local government reorganization Plymouth was downgraded from County Borough to District Council status – a sad come-down for the largest city west of Bristol (no doubt Drake did a further twist in his grave). Matters of education, libraries, social services, transport planning, etc. are now handled by the County Council at Exeter – an illogical and wasteful situation. There have been hints that the present government would look sympathetically at a case for change in status 'at an appropriate time' – but we all know what credence can be given to politicians' promises.

It would be a pity to end this chapter on a sour note so before leaving Plymouth let's look at Saltram House, a delightful

*Where else would you find such a view? As seen from the top of the Civic Centre, a tree-lined grassy bank sweeps away to the brow of the Hoe. Beyond, the Sound with Staddon Heights away on the left. Just pause to imagine the many and varied craft that have sailed across this expanse of water over the years.*

National Trust property at Plympton, within the city boundaries. So many of Britain's stately homes appear to have been built in a spasm of aristocratic upmanship – keeping up with the Jones's on a monumental scale – with heroic statues in the hall and stone gnome-ary in the garden. One feels that they were often built to impress rather than to be lived in.

Saltram could never be accused of this. Inside it really has the atmosphere of being a home. One could well imagine that the family have just gone out for a stroll and will be returning at any moment. Of a comfortable size, tastefully decorated and furnished, it is one of my favourite National Trust properties. The core of the

(Above) *Behind the classical, rather austere façade of Saltram House at Plympton, lies an interior full of character and rich in plasterwork and fine furniture.*

(Right) *Sun-dappled chestnuts, with a glint of water beyond. The River Plym at Plymbridge has been a favourite walking, fishing and lazing spot for generations of Plymouth people. It is now protected by the National Trust.*

building is Tudor, but with many alterations and additions. John and Lady Catherine Parker built the house much as we see it today in about 1750, but there were also additions in the nineteenth century. The salon and drawing-room were superbly decorated by Robert Adam in 1768 and the house contains a fine collection of English and French furniture. Sir Joshua Reynolds was a friend of the Parkers and frequently stayed at the house; many of his paintings hang on the walls. The gardens are pleasantly informal, with quiet walks through the woods lining the Plym estuary.

*The Yealm estuary splits near its mouth, with one arm going off to Steer Point and the other — seen here — leading to the delightful villages of Newton Ferrers and Noss Mayo.*

46

# CHAPTER TWO

# THE SOUTH HAMS

---

SOUTH HAMS – a puzzling name! Are they a band of half-baked itinerant actors? Or perhaps local radio amateurs? It's no wonder that 'non-Devonians' sometimes ask whether they should be eaten, listened to, sat on – or what? Perhaps the answer is to tour them leisurely, savouring the atmosphere of this delightful countryside which must be amongst the most beautiful and varied in Britain.

'Ham' derives from the old English word for low-lying meadowland, but this area also includes small harbours, precipitous cliffs and sandy beaches, together with a good sprinkling of thatch-and-whitewash cottages all characteristically set in tight-knit villages. In fact, it is most visitors' idea of typical Devonshire scenery, all contained within a comparatively small space.

Topographically, the bounds are difficult to define. By long-established custom they cover broadly the stretch of coast between the Rivers Yealm and Dart, and as far inland as the foothills of Dartmoor. The boundary of the South Hams District Council, set up in 1974, would not concur with this definition for their area takes in a broader span – all 450 square miles from the outskirts of Plymouth to the edge of Torbay. However, this is an administrative convenience and we are concerned with people and countryside, so let's keep to the time-honoured meaning.

For many years the South Hams have led a sheltered existence – a quiet backwater, out of the mainstream of tourist traffic and visited largely by local people and knowledgeable visitors who have returned year after year for sailing on the Kingsbridge Estuary, walking on the many coastal paths, or exploring the superb beaches and coves. All this could be changed by the 'tourist explosion' – to use current press jargon – now that the M5 motorway has been completed. The danger of 'over-visiting' spoiling the character of the countryside that urban holidaymakers are flocking to visit, and the attendant danger of commercial development in the wrong places, was recognized by the Devon County Council some years ago. In 1971 a booklet was published entitled 'The Motorway into Devon – The Challenge'. This summed up the views of the various council committees and presented a broad outline for tourist development within the county.

The South Hams was designated an 'Area of Restraint' – that is, a "coastal area where conservation of the existing landscape is a priority, although part of their function is the provision of quiet recreation and countryside experience". In contrast to this, the 'South Devon Riviera', a composite name for the stretch of coast from Exmouth to Brixham, became a 'Holiday Expansion Area' – described as "a coastal area where expansion of the holiday trade, including catering for day-trippers, should be encouraged, with suitable qualifications where appropriate". North Devon's 'Golden Coast', a somewhat glamorized name for the coastline between Westward Ho! and Ilfracombe, became a similar area, but with greater emphasis on the self-catering type of holiday.

The thinking behind all this is that people are coming to Devon in large numbers anyway, so to retain the character of the many attractive – and vulnerable – areas and to preserve the existing landscape, there must be positive promotion of other areas. If this smacks a little of 'let the devil take the hindmost', it is at least positive recognition that tourism is now one of Devon's largest industries – if not *the* largest.

But enough of other areas for the moment, for with luck – and good management – the South Hams will retain its unique character for many years to come. Its coastline – all forty miles or so – is indented by the estuaries of the Rivers Yealm, Erme, Avon and Dart, plus the huge enclosed tidal lake that forms the Kingsbridge Estuary, the Yealm is the odd man out – the Erme, Avon and Dart all rise high in the uplands of Dartmoor, but the infant Yealm sets off on its winding course not far from Cornwood, on the edge of the moor. Nevertheless, it has something in common with the Dart – both reach the sea through rocky inlets between steep cliffs, while the others end their travels against sandy beaches.

The entrance to the Yealm estuary forms a fine sheltered harbour, small in size, but providing moorings and anchorage for pleasure craft of every conceivable type. The twin villages of Newton Ferrers and Noss Mayo face each other across a creek which dries out at low tide to reveal the causeway connecting the two.

Like so many other coastal villages, just above the high-water mark, and at the bottom of a steep hill, are the original fishermen's cottages. Some are still owned by local people, others have been 'modernized' to become rather arty but attractive homes. The remainder can be grouped under the rather nebulous heading of 'holiday homes'.

High on the hillside are the more expensive houses – a sort of 'upper-crust' commuting suburb of Plymouth. At present, including the several hotels, there is a nice balance – the holidaymakers with their boats act as a leavening without overloading the facilities available. Fortunately, the holiday homes are not sufficiently numerous for Newton and Noss to become ghost villages in the winter. In August they are certainly alive, for the popular regatta is sheer good-humoured enjoyment for all. Scenically, one could not ask for a better composition – blue water, multicoloured dinghy sails, colour-washed cottages, and Noss's mellow old church tower looking down in the background.

Inland, the estuary is a quiet place, a bird-haunted, tree-lined inlet with Yealmpton standing close to its head. In Yealmpton's main street is an old thatched cottage – now a restaurant – which is said to be Mother Hubbard's Cottage in the nursery rhyme. Sarah Martin who wrote the rhyme in 1804 lived at Kitley House, a mile or so away, and Mother Hubbard is thought to have been the housekeeper there at the time.

St Bartholomew's Church was redesigned by Butterfield in 1850 and is interesting for the local marble used in its decoration – this is a form of polished limestone from nearby Kitley. The pillars are inlaid with alternate sections of black and grey marble with striking effect. Tucked away in a corner of the church are the old village stocks, kept there I assume as a convenient storage place and not as a salutary warning to the congregation!

From Yealmpton it is only a short distance to Mothecombe,

at the mouth of the Erme. A hamlet of cob and thatch cottages lines the road to Mothecombe House, a fine Queen Anne building with a hipped roof. For good measure, there are two sandy beaches here – the one nearest to the house is private but is, in fact, open to the public most of the time. The other, around the pine-covered headland, dries out at low water and by crossing a knee-deep stream one can reach Wonwell on the opposite side of the estuary. Be careful not to be caught by the returning tide – the grooves and gullies torn into the sand bear witness to the force of currents here!

Inland again is Modbury, a pleasant small market town, or I suppose, to be strictly accurate, large village. The main Plymouth–Kingsbridge road runs down its steep, narrow main street, with a sharply angled corner at the bottom. Streaks of paint on the wall show that this catches many an unwary driver. Yet it is a pity that you can spare only a fleeting glance if you value life, limb and coachwork, for Modbury is worth looking at more closely. Its houses with slate-hung fronts are typical South Devon buildings and these, together with the sixteenth-century half-timbered Exeter Inn and a score or so later additions, make up a delightfully informal, haphazard jumble of styles. These houses were designed and built *by* real people, *for* real people to live in, unlike the dreary, featureless, slab-sided, out-of-scale, 'accommodation units' of the large towns. Can we wonder that such an environment produces dreary, featureless people! We pay a high price for the uniformity beloved by architects nowadays; human nature demands choice, variety and individual expression. If these basic needs are ignored, should we be surprised if boredom breeds vandalism and crime?

The well-worn pavement climbs the hill in a series of leaps and bounds – a few steps up and then a slope – repeated to the top. In Brownston Street there are more interesting old buildings, including the early Victorian Traine House with its long, one-storeyed colonnade of double columns. Opposite is a conduit dated 1708, with a bulbous top and pinnacles. St George's Church stands high

*The tide-ripped beach at Mothecombe. A dramatic picture and a warning not to trifle with the currents when bathing here.*

above the town and its characteristic steeple is a landmark for many miles around. Much of the body of the church is believed to date from the fourteenth century, although some rebuilding took place after it was struck by lightning in 1621.

Bigbury-on-Sea is one of the most popular beaches in the area – sadly marred in parts by developments quite out of keeping with the area. A huge and very ugly car park adjoins a superb beach of fine yellow sand with rock pools. The National Trust has established a toe-hold on one of the headlands and with luck will eventually be able to protect more of this glorious coastline.

Offshore, Burgh Island dominates the view. This is a miniature of St Michael's Mount in Cornwall, which in itself is a replica of Mont St Michel in Brittany. On the summit there was once even a chapel dedicated to St Michael, but all traces have now gone. At low tide, the walk to the island involves a pleasant stroll across a spit of sand, but as the tide returns in a pincer movement this can become a treacherous mass of seething water, full of cross currents. To reach the hotel on the island at high tide one rides on a strange 8-foot high platform with seats, which is mounted on a caterpillar-wheeled tractor-type base. If this Neptune's Chariot were allowed on the public highway I wonder what licence category it would come under – motorized grandstand, perhaps, or amphibious farm machinery!

By far the best way to see this coast is to walk it from end to end along the coastal footpath, but assuming one is tied to four wheels, at this point it is necessary to turn inland to circumnavigate another estuary – that of the Avon. There is a short cut along the edge of the reed-flanked mudbanks, but keep an eye on the incoming tide, for the road is below the high-tide line for much of the way.

At the head stands Aveton Gifford (pronounced locally Awton Jiffard). The village had a fine thirteenth-century church, but – and it is difficult to imagine a more unlikely target – it was virtually destroyed in a 'hit and run' air raid in 1943. It has since been rebuilt within the shell and the stone has already mellowed sufficiently for it to merge into this gentle landscape almost as well as its predecessor.

Crossing the river on a long embankment-cum-bridge and climbing steep Aveton Gifford hill, we come to a junction. Here

*Modbury, a fine example of Devon slate-hung houses and a delightful hotch-potch of styles, with well-worn steps perfectly in keeping with the rest.*

there is a choice of routes, left to Kingsbridge, straight on to Salcombe, right to Bantham. Let's first turn right, down to the sand dunes, long beach, and jagged rocks of Bantham. In the background is Bigbury, on the opposite bank of the Avon which here flows swiftly through a narrow cleft in the headlands; inland it widens into a sandy estuary backed by the chequered pattern of fields.

The dunes offer countless small hollows, ideal for sunbathing on a windy summer day, but unfortunately sand is spreading rapidly inland over rough pasture once cropped by sheep. The grass is fighting a losing battle and attempts have been made at re-establishment by planting closely spaced clumps of new roots in fenced-off areas, but so far without a great deal of success.

There are many tales told of smuggling and wrecking on West

*A small boy and his dog taking the tidal road, a short cut between Bigbury and Aveton Gifford.*

Country coasts and the same stories appear in many places under different guises. The 'wrecking parson' is a favourite. One Sunday as the parson was preaching to his flock, a man who had been keeping lookout on the cliff crept quietly into the back of the church and signalled to him. Without pausing in his sermon, parson stepped down from the pulpit and walked down the aisle, shedding his surplice as he went. Having reached the door, he turned to his congregation and said, "My Christian brethren, there's a wreck on the shore. Let's all start fair!" And he headed his flock out of the church at the double!

Perhaps the attitude of all those who lived near the coast is best summed up in this 'prayer': "We pray thee Lord, not that wrecks shall happen, but that if any wrecks do happen, Thou wilt guide them to . . . [wherever], for the benefit of the poor inhabitants." There were also West Country highwaymen, and visitors have been heard to comment, after paying car-parking fees at some of

*Sun highlights the incoming tide at Bigbury as it sweeps up in two arcs to surround and cut off Burgh Island in the background. At low tide it is a pleasant walk to the island across the sand.*

Devon's towns and resorts, that old traditions die hard!

Hope Cove had a reputation for smuggling – perhaps unde-served – but its lonely setting against the sombre bulk of Bolt Tail gives credence to some of the tales. Today it is a delightful place. The cliffs and beach – particularly towards Thurlestone – are a deep red. Outer Hope is a small bay, enclosed by a concrete break-water giving shelter to several crabbers. Inner Hope, a hundred or so yards inland and snug in a cleft in the cliffs, consists of a square of fishermen's cottages, all thatch, whitewash, cobbles and roses round the door.

Between Hope Tail and Bolt Head is some of the finest cliff scenery in Devon. Soar Mill Cove – originally and unfairly called Sewer Mill – is typical. This is a dramatic cleft in the high cliffs, with a fine sandy beach at the bottom. To get there involves a drive down a narrow unsurfaced road, followed by a walk across several fields, so the beach is in little danger of becoming overcrowded. This is let's-sit-down-and-have-a-rest country. After climbing the steep cliffs you can regain your breath at the top, amidst banks of yellow gorse alive with bees. Lying on the soft, short grass, listen-ing to the muffled rhythm of the waves breaking 100 feet below and focusing on the lazy gyrations of a gull, one is far from the snarled-up, traffic-choked roads inland. The only reminder per-haps is the long, low shape of an oil tanker way off on the horizon and heading up channel.

The cliff path alternately climbs and plunges on its tortuous way to Bolt Head and Salcombe. At Bolt Head it clings precariously to the cliff side amidst jagged rock outcrops. Around the headland is Salcombe Castle (also called Fort Charles) which was erected by Henry VIII as part of the south-west coastal defences. In the Civil War it was the last place to hold out for the King; after a four-month-long siege it finally surrendered with honour and the defenders marched out carrying their weapons. All that remains today is a rather dilapidated round tower still standing forlorn guard over the harbour entrance.

*The coastline between Bolt Head and Salcombe is wild and windswept. These saw-edged rocks line the path that winds like a drunken serpent between the two places.*

*A view from the path through National Trust headlands which eventually leads to Prawle Point. The beach is Mill Bay, with Salcombe town across the water.*

Salcombe's buildings are more harmonious than striking, although the narrow streets have character, with ships' chandlers, boatyards and restaurants. The whole town has a flavour of the sea and it earns its living by catering for the needs of yachtsmen, both local and 'foreigners'. Thank heavens it has not yet succumbed to the rash of cheap souvenir shops so often found in waterside towns.

It is the home of the Island Cruising Club, which was founded in 1951 to provide cruising under sail in a fleet of craft jointly owned by members. Their craft, particularly *Provident*, a former Brixham trawler, and *Hoshi*, a 50-ton gaff-schooner, are a magnificent sight

*It's not only Devon's roads that are congested! Here dinghies jostle for space at Salcombe's pontoon landing stage, and most are only tenders to larger craft moored further out.*

as they sail down the harbour at the beginning of a week or fortnight's cruise.

One could well call Kingsbridge the capital of the South Hams, a bustling town with steep main street and a 'lived-in' atmosphere. Unlike so many other West Country towns it doesn't put up the shutters when the last summer visitor leaves – on the contrary its shops are small enough to offer a personal service and to stock the hundred and one small items completely unobtainable in the super stores of the larger towns. Its shops and businesses serve the needs of a large community, with a catchment area covering most of the South Hams.

The name of Kingsbridge is said to derive from an incident involving an unnamed Saxon king, who at an unspecified date was travelling through the area and reached the Dodbrooke – presumably a wider stream in those days – and was unable to cross. The local populace, forming a human bridge, carried him shoulder-high across the stream. Hence the name. Whether the story is true or not, there was certainly a bridge here in the tenth century, linking the two royal estates of Alvington and Chillington, and it would be logical for the point where they met to be called Kingsbridge.

In 1219, the Abbot of Buckfast obtained a market for the township and by 1238 it was a borough. Surprisingly, although several miles from the open sea, from the fourteenth to the nineteenth century it was quite a busy port, exporting wool from the surrounding countryside and tools from its foundry. It also had small ship-building, textile, flour and brewing industries. However, it is best known for its connection with porcelain. William Cookworthy, who discovered china clay in England and made the first English porcelain, was born here in 1705. Some of his porcelain figures and other items can be seen in the City Museum at Plymouth.

The Shambles – or Market Arcade – in Fore Street was built in 1585 and refaced in 1796. The upper floor extends over the pavement, supported on solid granite piers, and above is a squat steeple, surmounted by a four-faced clock. The whole building is visible for the length of the street – up and down – and forms a most interesting central feature amongst the other slate-hung buildings.

*Kingsbridge Creek, nowadays a peaceful scene. But several hundred years ago there would have been great waterside activity, for this was a busy port.*

St Edmund's Church, also in Fore Street, is probably best known for the oft-quoted epitaph on a tombstone in the chancel wall.

> Here lie I at the Chancel Door,
> Here lie I because I'm Poor,
> The further in the More you'll Pay,
> Here lie I as warm as they.

This philosophical memorial — no doubt a dig at the rich of his day — was written by Richard Phillips, a cooper, who is said to have enjoyed reciting it to his friends until he died in 1793. On my last visit I found the churchyard gates firmly padlocked. Perhaps a sign on the wall forbidding the exercising of dogs in the graveyard had some bearing on this! It is becoming only too common to find

*Arguably this is one of the finest views in the county. Looking from Start Point up the coast, past the haunted village of Hallsands, to Beesands in the next bay, then Slapton and Strete way off in the distance.*

church doors locked against vandals, but this seems to be something new; perhaps another indication of declining standards!

At the bottom of the hill there are attractive walks alongside a wide expanse of sparkling water – or, if the tide should happen to be out, a moonscape of black mud. I would advise a visit at high water, if only to take a boat trip from the quayside down this very beautiful estuary. Another pleasure would be to take tea aboard the *Compton Castle*, the last of the old Torbay paddle steamers, now moored permanently at the head of the creek and serving a dual role as open-air cafe and floating museum.

From Kingsbridge it is only a few miles to Start Point ('Start' comes from 'steort', meaning 'tail' and referring to the shape of the headland). The white-painted lighthouse with its attendant huddle of buildings stands four-square on this exposed and jagged promontory, a welcome landmark to many a sailor or yachtsman making for the shelter of Start Bay or Dartmouth. If possible, walk this coast on a winter's day, with the sea-smell in the air and the taste of salt-spray on your lips, flung high from the boiling waves far below. The wind shrieks through the rocky outcrops while eddies fret at the gorse bushes and tear petulantly at the tufts of coarse grass. A foaming grey-green sea merges at the horizon into a lack-lustre sky, across which packs of gulls fly swiftly, wind-driven inland against their will.

Hallsands is a haunted place, haunted by the fishermen and their families who lived here until 1917, when most of the village was washed away in a storm. A protective bank of shingle had been dredged from the beach and this altered the wave pattern. An elderly lady – Miss Pettyjohn – continued for many years to live defiantly on in her cottage at the waves' edge. When she died, her home gradually crumbled and joined the formless walls of other buildings, all that is left of the former village. A new village was built on the headland, high above the sea.

Back on the A379 again, stop at Torcross and climb the almost hidden cliff path in front of the hotel, past an old concrete pillbox, and you will find a breathtaking view – miles of what appears to be golden sand, but is in fact a bank of pebbles varying in size from tennis balls to peanuts. At low tide there is also some sand. The view stretches away for the length of Start Bay, almost to Dartmouth in the far distance. In fine weather this is an ideal place for small boats, rubber dinghies and the other paraphernalia that we all take to the beach, but take care if there should be a heavy sea: the beach shelves steeply in steps and there can be a vicious undertow.

Climb further up the cliff path and the view will open to take in Slapton Ley, a vast freshwater lake which is a nature reserve and the home of coots, moorhens, reed warblers and others, together with several families of swans. To the left is the lake, to the right the sea, and the road runs straight as a die down the centre on an embankment.

(Left) *This is not sand — more's the pity — but pebbles of varying sizes. The view is of Slapton Sands from Torcross, and the Ley — a freshwater nature reserve — lies behind the beach to the left.* (Above) *Slapton Ley.*

Halfway along this embankment is an obelisk, the plaque on which speaks eloquently for itself:

> This Memorial was presented by the United States Army Authorities to the people of the South Hams who generously left their homes and their lands to provide a battle practice area for the successful assault in Normandy in June 1944. Their action resulted in the saving of many hundreds of lives and contributed in no small measure to the success of the operation. The area included the villages of Blackawton, Chillington, East Allington, Slapton, Stokenham, Strete and Torcross, together with many outlying farms and houses.

This was a no-holds-barred practice area. Live ammunition was

used for the practice landings, and the odd landmine still turns up on the beach from time to time. I had reason to visit the area in 1944, after the troops had moved out but before the displaced people moved back. As I remember it, it was an eerie experience, driving through deserted villages with not even a domestic cat or dog to be seen. Fields were overgrown with no cattle to crop the grass. I recall seeing a riot of self-seeded shoulder-high flowers in the garden of a thatched cottage whose front door hung askew on broken hinges; apple trees with the fruit unpicked on the branches and even a vine full of grapes in a deserted greenhouse. Yet not a sound was to be heard, except for the birds, the first to resume residence.

There was the ever-present danger of being blown up, for the area was littered with the equipment of a mock but deadly 'war' in which there had been many casualties. As witness to the 'street fighting' the church at Stokenham had its windows blown out and there were bullet holes in the wall of the pub opposite. Today all is calm and Stokenham is one of the pleasantest 'thatch and whitewash' villages in the county.

About Dartmouth, Daniel Defoe wrote in his eighteenth-century *Tour Through Great Britain*: "The opening into Dartmouth Harbour is not broad, but the Channel deep enough for the biggest ship in the Royal Navy. The narrow entrance is not much above half a mile, when it opens and makes a basin or harbour able to receive 500 sail of ships of any size, and where they may ride with the greatest safety, even as in a mill-pond or wet dock."

Today, certainly some of the smallest ships of the Royal Navy – sailing craft from the Royal Naval College – pass frequently in and out of the harbour entrance, but it would be a tight squeeze for an aircraft carrier!

On the steep hillsides rise tiers of houses like a multicoloured

*This obelisk, standing starkly against the setting sun, is half way along the beach at Slapton. It was presented by the United States Army Authorities in thanks to the people who evacuated the area during the war.*

*A French force landed here at Blackpool Sands in the reign of Henry IV, with the intention of attacking Dartmouth, but they were decisively defeated. Visitors today can be sure of a rather warmer welcome!*

iced cake, but there is nothing frivolous about Dartmouth – these are solid seafarers' houses, built on the profits of overseas trade. The sea-going tradition is obvious in the crests on the buildings and the boatlike windows. The town grew from two small settlements – Hardness and Clifton – which were originally separated by an inlet of the estuary, called Mill Pool. By the thirteenth century these had combined and the name Dartmouth came to be used. The inlet was filled in and is represented today by the flat, low-lying land in the centre of the town. In 1147, this magnificent deep-water harbour saw the departure of 164 vessels on the

*A fine old pub – the Tradesmen's Arms – thatch and whitewash cottages: the essence of a Devonshire village. This is Stokenham, near Torcross, one of the villages evacuated in the last war to allow American troops to practise landing under battle conditions.*

69

Second Crusade and in 1190 Richard Coeur de Lion gathered here another large fleet for the Third Crusade to the Holy Land.

As a result of Henry II's marriage in 1152, Bordeaux and the south-west provinces of France became possessions of the English crown and this gave a great stimulus to trade. Totnes cloth and wool from all over the South Hams was exported through the port and the merchants grew rich on the wine trade. John Hawley was one of the greatest of these and is probably the 'Schipman of Derthmute' mentioned in Chaucer's *Canterbury Tales,* for the poet visited the port in 1373 in his capacity as Inspector of Customs, and met Hawley.

In the reign of Richard II, during one of the periodic skirmishes with the French, the inhabitants received word of an assembled invasion fleet. These merchants and semi-legal privateers, commanded by Hawley, "manned forth a few ships at their own peril and charge" and entering the Seine destroyed the French vessels, returning laden with plunder.

It was Hawley too who first fortified the entrance to the harbour in 1388 with a rock-cut ditch and curtain wall. Later, agreement was reached between the King and burgesses over payment for a more elaborate fortification including a "cheyne sufficient in length and strength to streche and be laid overthwarte or a travers the mouth of the haven of Dartmouth". The castle still stands today, an attractive sea-mark and an indivisible part of the group that includes the small church of St Petrox and the tower named Gallants Bower – a redoubt in the Civil War. Dartmouth enjoyed a further wave of prosperity in the sixteenth century from the Newfoundland cod fishing trade and from the export of cloth –

*(Left) Daniel Defoe commented on the entrance to Dartmouth Harbour when he passed this way in the eighteeenth century. It is still busy today, with a continuous stream of small boats sailing past the Castle and Gallants Bower.*

*(Overleaf) The Inner Harbour at Dartmouth. The still water reflects a delightful medley of boats and houses, the latter in an uninhibited mixture of styles – including the famous Butter Walk, a corner of which can be seen to the right.*

mostly made at Ashburton. Many of the solid gabled houses date from this time and the success of this trade enabled a new quay to be built.

At Bayards Cover there is a very attractive group of waterside houses of differing styles, as Professor Nikolaus Pevsner says: "not of high intrinsic merit but not easily matched as a whole". This cobbled quayside appeared in many episodes of the first BBC TV series 'Onedin Line', when suitable props and carefully contrived camera angles transformed it from a Liverpool dock scene to a West Indies harbour (complete with slaves), and many other locations.

At one time Dartmouth had the distinction of being the only town in the country with a railway booking office, but no railway! Passengers bought their tickets in the office on the quayside and then boarded a ferry to reach the station at Kingswear on the opposite side of the river. British Rail abandoned the line many years ago and it is now operated by a private company – but more about this later.

Another casualty of rising costs and falling trade has been the Dart steamers which for many years operated a passenger service from Dartmouth to Totnes at the head of navigation. This was a magnificent trip, particularly if one returned by rail or road. Fortunately, it is still possible to travel up the Dart by launch, in slightly less style.

Two ferries carry cars across the river. The Upper Ferry is the more conventional – a floating deck with paddle wheels which adds a slightly Mississippi-like air to the river. The Lower Ferry is merely a pontoon holding half a dozen cars and propelled by a launch with its bow fastened to the centre point. This strange arrangement actually works well, the boat swinging on its axis and changing direction at the end of each trip.

One could go on and on about Dartmouth. The Pilgrim Fathers' ships *Speedwell* and *Mayflower* left from here before being beaten into Plymouth by bad weather. Thomas Newcomen, 'Father of the Steam Engine', was born here and anticipated Watt by more than sixty years. Dartmouth has been called the 'Cradle of the Navy' and until 1905 all officer cadets for the Royal Navy were trained in the *Britannia*, a ship moored in the harbour; she was broken up when the Royal Naval College opened.

But shall we let Defoe have the final word on dining in Dart-mouth, for he was fond of good food, a sort of cross between an early Egon Ronay and a Consumer Research Unit! He had been taken out in a boat by an acquaintance and, returning to find the town "all in a kind of uproar", asked what it was all about.

The matter was that a great shoal – or, as they call it, a "school" – of pilchards, came swimming, with the tide of flood, directly out of the sea into the harbour. My friend whose boat we were in, told me that this was a surprise which he would have been very glad of if he could have had a day or two's warning, for he might have taken 200 tun of them. We sent our servant to the quay to buy some, who for a half-penny brought us seventeen, and, if he would have taken them, might have had as many more for the same money.

He goes on, "With these we went to dinner; the cook at the inn broiled them for us, which is their way of dressing them, with pepper and salt, which cost us about a farthing, so that the two of us and a servant dined – and at a tavern, too – for three farthings, dressings and all." I wonder what the cost would be today!

*Buckland Abbey, a thirteenth-century Cistercian abbey. Lived in by Sir Richard Grenville, then bought by Sir Francis Drake, it is now owned by the National Trust and leased to Plymouth Corporation as a Naval Museum.*

# CHAPTER THREE

# DARTMOOR

---

THERE CAN BE few areas in Britain so fiercely fought over as this expanse of wild country, with its tors, bogs and peat-stained streams. No, these are not historic battles fought with cannon and musket over the rolling moor, but actions of more recent times with the adversaries locked in combat in the columns of the Press, on television, or arguing their various cases in committee rooms.

Preservationists are opposed to the Services using the moor for training, farmers attempt to restrict public access, everyone claims that someone else is interfering with grazing rights or ancient monuments, mining companies dig huge holes in the ground and create artificial mountains from the china clay spoil, water authorities attempt to flood valleys to keep up with the apparently insatiable demand for more reservoirs, there are disputes over public versus private transport – and so it goes on. One wonders how the sheep and ponies manage to live in harmony together!

As an illustration of the amazing complexities of moorland politics, at the latest of a long series of public enquiries into the Services' use of the moor for training, Devon County Council supported the Services, while the Dartmoor National Parks Committee – its protégé – aligned with the Dartmoor Preservation Association and other amenity organizations in their efforts to remove, or at least restrict, the Services. The preservation of the moor is a subject on which passions are easily aroused; on a subject about as emotive as fox-hunting it is difficult to present an unbiased view, but I will do my best!

Dartmoor is all things to all men. To the average family man it is a place to drive on a Sunday afternoon – as a change from the

*No one would dispute that the mining of china clay on Dartmoor is an environmental disaster, but the winning of minerals has gone on for centuries and much of the clay is a vital export. This huge pit, reputed to be the largest in Europe, is at Lee Moor.*

beach. He expects to park his car and perhaps picnic close by, with maybe a not too energetic stroll to a nearby tor or lake. The enthusiastic walker with compass in his hand and haversack on his back (and perhaps a lightweight tent) sets off for the wilder parts and thinks nothing of covering twenty miles or so. Many organized groups ramble, with greater or lesser degrees of energy and dedication, over large areas, for the pure pleasure of walking, or to visit ancient monuments and landmarks.

The annual 'Ten Tors' race is a classic example of the sensible use of this wild open country for adventure and initiative training. Teams of youngsters from youth clubs, etc. set out to hike their way across the moor calling at predetermined marshalling points and, as the name implies, taking in ten tors *en route*.

The Services regard the moor as ideal training terrain where live

*Burrator Lake with Sheeps Tor in the background. This is a man-made reservoir, brought into use in 1898, and one of the few on the moor that has not caused controversy. All agree that this delightful expanse of water in its setting of tors and woodlands is a practical and aesthetic success.*

ammunition can be used to simulate battle conditions; they hold on jealously to land acquired more than 100 years ago and say that they cannot find other suitable firing ranges elsewhere in the country.

The huge china-clay pits in the Lee Moor area, together with their associated spoil heaps and settlement tanks, are an environmental disaster on a monumental scale — a preservationist's nightmare! On the other side of the coin, the winning of minerals from the moor is as old as history. Vast quantities of china clay are exported, all of which helps the country's balance of payments. Also the industry — including subsidiary plants for block-making, etc. — is responsible for many jobs in an area where work is hard to find. By the very nature of the industry, there will always be pressure to expand and it will take a great deal of courage on the part of a planning authority – local or national – to eventually say "No further into the National Park".

As though to underline the point, hardly had I finished writing that sentence than it was announced that permission had been given for a huge area of Shaugh Moor to be used for the tipping of waste. Although all local councils were opposed to the scheme, to withdraw planning permission given some years ago could well have cost in the region of a million pounds in compensation payments to the company.

Water is always a bone of contention. About the only reservoir universally accepted as an improvement to the landscape is Burrator and that probably because it was built as long ago as 1898, flooding 117 acres and several hill farms in the process. The small granite dam has mellowed over the years and this gem of a lake has banks covered in rhododendron and azalea bushes, and an encircling road from which to enjoy the view.

Not so easily accepted was the Avon Dam built in 1954 on a more exposed part of the moor – and bitterly contested was the Meldon reservoir scheme (only completed in 1973) which flooded an attractive valley to provide more water for North Devon. Swincombe, near Princetown, has been considered since 1970 for another reservoir and this scheme has run into widespread opposition. Although the site has been turned down as unsuitable, the 1976 drought may well cause second thoughts.

The chief opponent of exploitation in any form is the Dartmoor Preservation Association – one of the most influential amenity societies in the country. Its efforts over the years have prevented the worst excesses and made people think about Dartmoor – their Dartmoor – and consider how the future of this wild country should be safeguarded, so that the solitude and challenge may still be there for their children and future generations to enjoy.

If all these conflicting interests make the moor sound overcrowded, there are 365 square miles in the National Park – which was created in 1951 – and many more miles of open countryside on the fringes. But enough of politics, let's look at the moor itself which has survived remarkably unscathed because of – or perhaps in spite of – the plethora of bodies responsible for its well-being.

Dartmoor is incomparable, for there is nowhere else quite the same in Britain. The granite tors which are such a dramatic feature of the skyline are unique and few other moorland areas can equal the beauty of its wooded valleys and peat-stained streams. Probably spring and autumn are the best times to see the moor – in the heat of summer the peaty soil dries out and heather and gorse lose their lustre. Early in the year the grass is fresh underfoot, young ferns are breaking through and the gorse is a mass of vivid yellow flowers. In the autumn, ferns turn first to gold and then a russet hue. The slopes of beech and oak trees – Spitchwick is a good example – run the gamut of autumn colours from vivid green to deep red.

Two roads bisect the moor like a pair of scissors, the B3212 and the A384, with an upland plateau on each side, while the several roads passing through Tavistock–Okehampton–Dunsford–Ashburton–Ivybridge–Yelverton serve to encircle the

*The southern moor is softer and less rugged than the higher northern part. This view of Sheeps Tor from Ringmoor Down typifies the semi-cultivated edge with small fields petering out as the ground rises, and scattered small cottages. The superb cloudscape is also Dartmoor at its best.*

National Park. The southern moor is the softer, less rugged part, but before exploring this it is well worth while detouring a mile or so outside the National Park boundary to look at Buckland Abbey, near Yelverton.

This was founded in 1278 by Amicia, Countess of Devon, as a Cistercian House. At the Dissolution of the Monasteries the Abbey and its lands passed to Sir Richard Grenville who considerably altered the original building. In 1581 it was bought by Sir Francis Drake – who was born less than ten miles away – and he used it as his home and country retreat whenever he was in England. It remained in the possession of Drake's ancestors until comparatively recently – 1947, in fact – when the Abbey was acquired by the National Trust. With admirable foresight they leased it to Plymouth Corporation as a Naval Museum which is now filled with Drake relics, including his famous drum.

Also housed in the building is a folk museum with a fine collection of old farm implements, etc. When one considers that the Cistercian monks once owned 20,000 acres in the surrounding district and were enthusiastic farmers and sheep breeders, it is only fitting that this tradition should be represented in addition to the more stirring exhibits in the Naval Gallery. In the latter, above the fireplace can be seen Drake's coat of arms, while the clarion-trumpet badges of the Grenvilles are included in the corners of a fireplace in another room. Close to the Abbey is a magnificent tithe barn, hardly changed over the years. It takes little imagination to see its huge interior – 154 feet long by 28 feet wide and 40 feet high – filled with produce that the monks had won from their lands.

In 1590, Drake was the driving force behind the building of a leat to supply Plymouth with water. The legend that he rode on horseback from Head Weir the twenty-seven miles or so into Plymouth and commanded the water to follow him serves to illustrate the awe in which he was held after his success against the Armada. An ancient account gives another, rather more down-to-earth, description:

> Here [at the River Meavy, near Sheepstor] the river is taken out of the olde river and carried 448 paces through mightie rockes which was thought impossible to carrie water through. From the first taking in of

Drake built the first leat, seen above at Roborough Down, to bring water to Plymouth. In later years as Devonport expanded she also wanted a reliable supply of fresh water and another leat was built (overleaf). It is still in regular use, but has now been diverted to feed Burrator Reservoir. The view is near Nun's Cross Farm.

the river, that is now brought into Plimmouth (as it is carried everie waie to geat the vantage of the hilles) is by measure 27 miles after 1,000 paces to a mile and fyve foot a pace.

Today, we would call this a contour canal or leat, with a gentle fall for most of its distance. It remained Plymouth's main source of fresh water for more than three centuries, and although most has been built over within the city boundaries its serpentine path can still be traced across the moor to the source near Sheepstor.

Meavy village close by is best known for its fine old oak tree said to have existed at the time of King John and to be more than 800 years old. Today it is showing its age, its lightning-split trunk being supported by several timber trusses. In the churchyard is a philosophical epitaph to the village blacksmith who died on 18 April 1826, aged eighty years:

> My sledge and hammer both declin'd,
> My bellows too have lost their wind,
> My fire extinct, my forge decay'd,
> My coal is spent my irons gone,
> My nails are drove, my work is done.

An earlier blacksmith at Mary Tavy, near Tavistock, who appears to have been altogether a more rumbustious character, also has an unusual epitaph:

> Here buried were some years before,
> His two wives and five children more,
> One Thomas named, whose fate was such,
> To lose his life by wrestling much,
> Which may a warning be to all,
> How they into such pastimes fall.

Following the B3212 we come to Princetown, bleakly situated on a ridge below North Hessary Tor. In winter, a sombre place of weathered granite and grey walls; an enclosed village whose life revolves around the prison that overshadows it. Warders' houses, prison buildings and shops mingle in the single main street – with incongruously a 'Dartmoor Pixie Shop' – and all are often lost in low banks of clinging mist.

Why should a village grow in such a desolate spot? The whole community was largely the creation of one man – Thomas Tyr-whitt – a local landowner and Member of Parliament, who farmed Tor Royal Estate nearby. He had powerful and influential friends, including the Prince Regent (hence the name Princetown), and in 1805, when the authorities became concerned about the number of French prisoners of war confined in hulks in the Hamoaze at Plymouth and began searching for a more suitable prison, Tyrwhitt suggested that it should be sited at Princetown. His idea was accepted and the new building was completed in 1810, at a cost of £200,000. Eventually the French prisoners were repatriated and the prison buildings became virtually derelict. A number of uses were considered and in 1850 they became a convict prison – a use that has continued until the present day.

In summer – like the swallows – the visitors return to Princetown. Their cars and bright clothes add a splash of colour as they photograph the prison – mostly from a discreet distance. Prison

*A grim setting for a sombre building, only relieved by the clouds scudding across the open moor. Princetown Prison was built in 1810 to house French prisoners of war and only later became a convict prison.*

*Everything in Meavy village is built of solid moorland granite and looks as though it will last for ever. No wonder it all seems timeless, for the fine old oak on the left is believed to have existed at the time of King John. Hence the name of the inn, the Royal Oak.*

working parties and holidaymakers eye each other as they pass in the street; two worlds, a sentence apart. It is said that on one occasion recently the text on the parish church notice board near the prison read: "THE LORD WILL SET YOU FREE TO BECOME ALL YOU OUGHT TO BE"! Ponies still gather in the square, scrounging titbits, if they can manage to bypass the cattle grids intended to keep them out.

Doubling back on the Tavistock road, we pass close to Vixen Tor with an outline like an old man's face. Actually, so legend tells us, this was the home of Vixana an evil witch who lived in a cave halfway up the precipitous south face. She hated everyone and was

*Vixen Tor, one of the most interesting rock piles on the moor. One side falls away precipitously to the valley below, while from different angles the face of an old man and of various animals can be discerned with a little imagination. No wonder there is a legend about the tor.*

a thoroughly unpleasant character all round. Her favourite pastime was to look out for unwary travellers on the path that skirted the base of the tor. As they reached a certain spot she would wave her stick and summon up a typical Dartmoor mist – damp, clinging and impenetrable. The poor unfortunate would stumble into the bog, to be sucked to his death with Vixana's evil laughter ringing in his ears.

Now it seems that elsewhere on the moor lived a fortunate young man with two rather unusual attributes. Firstly, he had the gift of astonishingly clear sight and the ability to see without hindrance through the thickest of mists; secondly, he possessed a ring which, when placed on his finger, made him totally invisible. Having heard about the evil ways of Vixana, in a very public-spirited manner he set off to investigate.

The witch was sitting crouched in her usual position when she saw the young man approaching. Cackling with glee, she summoned up a real pea-souper – but with his clear sight the young man walked steadily on along the path. Missing the usual frenzied cries, Vixana cleared the mist with a single swish of her stick, but where was her intended victim? The witch was puzzled and arming herself with another spell moved to the very edge of her ledge to see better what was happening below.

In the meantime the young man, wearing his ring and, of course, totally invisible, had made his way round to the other side of the tor. Quietly approaching Vixana, he caught her unawares and with a quick push sent her tumbling off her ledge, screaming and cursing, into the bog below. Thus Vixana received her comeuppance and thanks to the unnamed young man we can today safely tread the very pleasant path around the base of the tor.

At Tavistock, the River Tavy flows gently through The Meadows – low-lying parkland and recreation grounds – described in the Saxon *stoc* from which the town is said to have derived its name. A historic town this, situated at the confluence of several ancient trackways. In the tenth century a vast Benedictine Abbey was built here, but within ten years of its completion, it was burned to the ground by marauding Danish pirates who had sailed up the River Tamar. It was rebuilt to become even more powerful and in 1166 Henry I handed over the Manors of Tavistock and Milton Abbot to the Abbey. About the middle of the twelfth century the Abbot apportioned an area of 325 acres of Abbey lands on the north bank of the Tavy for a new district to be called the Borough of Tavistock.

As a centre for the rapidly developing mining industry in the surrounding district the town grew around the Abbey and was granted Stannary status in 1305. The inhabitants of town and Abbey lived alongside each other (although not always in complete harmony) until in 1539, at the Dissolution, the Abbot and his council of monks were forced to sign a deed surrendering the

Abbey and all its lands to Henry VIII. It was not long before the lead was stripped from the roof of the Abbey church and the stone-work plundered to provide building material for the townsfolk.

Today there are some remains – but not many – of one of the most powerful religious settlements in the south-west. These are scattered throughout the town and include a few fragments of wall in the grounds of the parish church, the curiously named 'Betsy Grimbals' tower in the grounds of the present vicarage, and several sections of wall and towers alongside the river.

The Dukes of Bedford spent their mining royalties developing and laying out the town in wide streets and squares with granite-faced no-nonsense public buildings. Alongside the Yelverton road they built 100 miners' dwellings – cottages of a standard well in advance of their time and arranged in a manner from which today's planners could learn a great deal.

The Tavistock Canal was cut between 1803 and 1817 largely using French prisoner-of-war labour, to carry mined ore from the Wheal Crowndale mine to Morwellham on the River Tamar. Boats weighing some 8 tons were lowered down a 240 foot inclined plane from the end of the canal to the great wharves below where sailing craft waited to be loaded with the valuable ore.

Only pleasure craft penetrate the river today and Morwellham has become a Centre for Recreation and Education. In spite of its pretentious title this is a fascinating and history-haunted place, where one may walk the old cobbled quays with their massive stone ballards, or watch a working water wheel – or if energetic, climb the path of the old inclined plane and walk the canal bank as far as the tunnel mouth.

Sir Francis Drake was born at Tavistock and lest anyone should forget, a statue confronts the visitor in the middle of the road as he

*Tavistock was founded in the tenth century when a Benedictine abbey was built here. Later it became a centre for the developing mining industry and grew prosperous as a Stannary town where metal was taken to be assayed. It is also the birthplace of Sir Francis Drake.*

The stark remains of Wheal Betsy pump house at Blackdown. A plaque on the wall tells the full story: "This ancient silver-lead mine was re-opened in 1806 and worked successfully for the next seventy years. The mine was worked by water power until 1868 when this building was erected to house a Cornish Beam Pumping Engine. Until its closure in 1877 all pumping, winding and crushing of ore was carried out by steam power." In 1967 the ruined engine house and stack were acquired and made safe by the National Trust as a memorial to the mining industry of Dartmoor.

*Postbridge, one of the old clapper bridges, which is crossed by thousands of visitors each year. It spans the East Dart River and is a very popular spot for picnics.*

approaches the town. This, incidentally, is the original of that which stands on Plymouth Hoe, a later copy.

There are many clapper bridges on the moor, crossing rivers and streams – Dartmeet, Bellever, Cherry Brook and others – but undoubtedly the most visited is at Postbridge. This structure of rough hewn granite slabs bears the feet of thousands of visitors every year. It probably dates from the thirteenth century as do most of the moorland bridges, and was used by travellers on foot and by packhorses.

Even more numerous are the granite crosses scattered across the

(Above) *The moor abounds in antiquities — menhirs, stone circles, burial mounds and the like. One particularly interesting feature is Grimspound, which probably dates from the Bronze Age. It is situated on the open moor only a short distance from the Postbridge–Moretonhampstead road. A stout stone wall encloses about twenty-four hut circles, one of which is shown above.*

(Right) *There are dozens of crosses on the moor, most marking ancient trackways. However, this one — Childe's Tomb, near Princetown — has a legend attached about a hunter and how he met his death on the lonely moor.*

moor and its perimeter. These were mostly used as 'signposts' by travellers in the Middle Ages. When walking the moor in bad weather it is easy to imagine how welcome a sight one of these must have been, looming up out of the mist in front of a weary wayfarer.

The 'Abbots Way' is a clearly defined route across the southern moor which very likely linked Buckfast Abbey to the east with the abbeys at Tavistock and Buckland. No doubt it was also used by

other travellers between villages and by miners walking to the scattered mineral workings on the moor; perhaps also for the cutting and carrying of peat for fuel. Certainly most of the old tracks were used for a variety of purposes, the most macabre probably being the Lich Way. Because the scattered farms around the Walla Brook came under the parish of Lydford, the dead had to be carried six miles or so over the moor and along this path for burial at Lydford church.

There are several legends about the old crosses, including one known as Childe's Tomb, at Fox Tor, near Princetown. Childe, it is said, owned extensive lands in the Plymstock area (near Plymouth), but was very fond of hunting alone on the moor in all weathers. One day he was caught in a blizzard far from any habitation on the edge of Fox Tor Mire. Eventually, realizing that he could not hope to reach shelter, in desperation he killed his horse, disembowelled it and climbed inside the carcase for warmth and shelter. Fearing that he would die, he wrote a note:

> They fyrst that fyndes and brings mee to my grave,
> The Priory of Plimstoke they shall have.

The storm continued unabated and days later Childe's frozen body was found and his death reported to the monks at Tavistock Abbey. They were determined that the body should be buried in the grounds of Tavistock Abbey church, but the monks of Plymstock had also, by then, heard of his death. As he was a Plymouth man – and fearful for the loss of their lands – they set out to abduct his body as it was being carried to Tavistock.

However, the Abbot at Tavistock received word of the ambush and by building a new bridge across the River Tavy at a higher point his monks avoided it. Because he succeeded by guile the new bridge became known as Guilebridge. This story may well be based on a true incident but the place now known as Childe's Tomb probably marks the spot where his body was found, not buried.

Moretonhampstead used to be known as the 'Capital of the Moor', but now it is a quiet market town with an impressive granite church and a striking row of seventeenth-century almshouses with a stone arcade. Nearby is Chagford, a large village (or small town) with a great deal of character. 'Chag' is an old dialect word for gorse. The community developed here as early as the twelfth century as a market centre for the surrounding moorland farms and later also became a centre for the tin mining industry. In 1305 it was made one of the three moorland Stannary towns to which miners brought their metal for assay and stamping.

It prospered for a while spinning wool for the weavers of East Devon until the woollen industry declined. Early in the twentieth century it became popular as a 'bracing' holiday resort for hikers and lovers of the countryside, visitors being conveyed from the G.W.R. station at Moretonhampstead by special bus.

Today it has the mellowness of a place that is no longer busy, but has not decayed. There is a fine old thatched and mullioned six-teenth-century inn – The Three Crowns – and an interesting church. It is particularly well served by small shops, including one calling itself an ironmonger's but like an outback wild west store, stocking everything of any conceivable use to the local com-munity. It is one of life's pleasures to browse through such country stores where everyone knows everyone else and service still mat-ters. Goods are stacked in glorious confusion: "Your fishing line is up on the top shelf, Bill – help yourself to the steps." "Yes Mrs B, carpet shampoo upstairs on the right, mind that broken stair on the way up." "Pint of peas? Certainly." All straight from a sack, none of this pre-packed nonsense here.

On the eastern perimeter of the moor there is a clutch of the most attractive villages in Devon – North Bovey, Lustleigh, Man-aton, Buckland-in-the-Moor, etc. North Bovey is superb, with thatched cottages set around a wooded village green and over-looked by a mellowed granite church. Buckland-in-the-Moor has a much-photographed huddle of thatched dwellings in a sheltered hollow and on the hill above an unusual clock memorial on the church tower. Instead of figures the hours are represented by let-ters making the words M-Y-D-E-A-R-M-O-T-H-E-R. Widecombe-in-the Moor is not far away. The famous song is commemorated by a stone plaque on the village green, but it is doubtful whether Uncle Tom Cobleigh and his old grey mare would nowadays find room to manoeuvre between the hundreds of cars that descend on the

The clock face on the church at Buckland-in-the-Moor is intended as a memorial and the hours are represented by letters making up the words 'My Dear Mother'.

place for the September Fair. Neither would he recognize the Fair, a sadly commercialized version of the original.

In the eastern section of the moor are also some of the most interesting tors. These volcanic exuberances stand out well against the rolling moorland and break the skyline in dramatic fashion. Haytor is easy to reach from a large car park by the roadside, up a very well beaten track. There are steps cut into the rock and it is easy to climb. From the top there is a magnificent panoramic view ranging over moor and countryside, with even a distant silvery glint from the sea, ten miles or so away, in the direction of Teignmouth.

Dartmoor granite has always been considered of a high quality for building purposes and in the early nineteenth century, with the prospect of a contract for London Bridge, George Templer of Stover House decided to construct a tramway to carry stone from the Haytor quarries to the terminal basin of the Stover Canal.

*Skittles on the village green at North Bovey, on the edge of Dartmoor.*

From here it could be carried on canal boats to the coast and then transported by sea. What better material to use for the track than the granite to be carried upon it? There was certainly plenty close at hand and who could wish for a harder wearing material. Blocks of varying lengths had a 3-inch flange cut in one face and were laid to give a gauge of 4 feet 3 inches. On this crude track ran flat-topped wagons carrying the slabs of granite; even points and sidings were provided, the key stones being pivoted to guide the wagons in the required direction.

The wagons ran downhill in groups of about twelve under their own weight and must have been a frightening spectacle lurching noisily down the uneven track. To return for another load, shafts were fitted to the empty wagons and these were pulled by teams of horses.

The tramway was opened in 1820 and many tons of granite were transported for use on London Bridge, the British Museum and other London buildings. During its lifetime demand gradually fell

*Like Postbridge, Haytor must groan under the weight of the many visitors who, each year, climb to the top for the magnificent view in all directions. With luck they will catch a glint of the sea, ten miles away. Climbers also use the sheer faces for practice in roping.*

*If you stumble over a section of shaped stone as you walk around Haytor, stop and have a closer look. It will probably be part of the tramway built to carry granite blocks from nearby quarries to the Stover Canal and thence by sea to London. Many famous London buildings are faced with Dartmoor granite.*

away and it finally closed in 1858. Many of the shaped slabs are still in place and the trackway can easily be traced – it crosses a minor road leading to Manaton, just off the Haytor–Bovey Tracey road.

Bowerman's Nose is an unusual granite stack – hardly a tor – quite illogically set on a bare hillside near Manaton. However, there is inevitably a legend to account both for its position and appearance – that of a man's face and body when viewed from the hill above. We are told that Bowerman was a hunter, a tall and powerful but kindly man, who roamed the moor with a pack of fine hounds. It seems that the area in which he hunted was unfortunately also used by the local witches for their Sabbaths. The

moorland people roundabout were, quite understandably, terri-
fied of the witches and gave them a very wide berth. Not so
Bowerman – he even taunted them and sometimes rode right
through their covens accompanied by his hounds, scattering them
cauldron over broomstick. Now the witches were not used to this
sort of treatment and decided on revenge.

One of their number had the useful ability of being able to turn
herself into a hare, and the next time Bowerman came that way she
set off in front of his pack. Over hill, tor and open moor went the
chase with the hare always just out of reach, until at last when
Bowerman and his pack were completely exhausted the hare
swerved aside and they thundered into a small depression in the
moor. Too late Bowerman realized that he had been ambushed for
there were all the other witches, armed with their most potent
combined spell. Alas, this was too strong for poor Bowerman and
he was turned into stone. There he sits today looking down from
his hillside over the country he loved to hunt.

Between Moretonhampstead and Okehampton lies Castle
Drogo, perched high on a rocky outcrop like a medieval fortress.
In fact, it was designed by Sir Edwin Lutyens for a Mr Julius
Drewe and built in the twenty years between 1910 and 1930. It is
an imaginative, romantic building, dominating the skyline, but
essentially it was intended as a large private house, designed for
family living. Through the granite-framed windows one looks
down into the wooded gorge of the River Teign while beyond is a
magnificent panoramic view of hills and tors. The property was
acquired by the National Trust in 1974 and is now open to the
public. There are some interesting paintings, tapestries and furniture.

Okehampton, on the very fringe of the northern moor, consists
primarily of one long main street, through which the A30 traffic
thunders on its way to Cornwall. On one side, at right angles to

*An unusual rock pile, set on a hillside with no apparent connection with
any other tor. Bowerman, we are told, was a hunter and this is his nose.
Could the legend that he was turned to stone on this spot be the answer?*

the main road, is an attractive glassed-over arcade of small shops, a quiet, pleasant place to browse away from the traffic. On the other side of the road a brave attempt is being made to repeat the theme of a small intimate shopping precinct, in a more modern idiom. Reconstituted stone and natural timber are used extensively and the layout is interesting with plenty of odd nooks, crannies and unusual vistas.

With whitewashed walls and timber framing the effect is part Spanish Mediterranean, part Old English, all overlaid with Dartmoor traditional. Perhaps surprisingly the result has character and presents an almost gay atmosphere in an otherwise rather sombre town. As with so many other small towns, Okehampton has had the foresight to place a large free car park alongside its shops. The larger cities may well come to regret their policies of high car parking charges as they find trade slipping away to the smaller, more convenient towns.

The ruins of Okehampton Castle surmount a grassy hummock a mile outside the town and seem to live permanently in a splint of scaffolding, an indication that they are being well cared for by the Department of the Environment. The ground and ruins have been extensively renovated and excavated. The site was at the confluence of several important routes and the castle came into being as a result of the Norman Conquest. Shortly after the Battle of Hastings, there was a rising in the south-west, centred on Exeter. This was suppressed and Baldwin FitzGilbert was appointed Sheriff of Devon. No doubt partly to overawe the local population, but also because several of Baldwin's manors were in this area, Okehampton was chosen as the site for a stronghold.

The defences in those days must have been primitive, but doubtless the mere presence of troops would have served to represent the King's authority. In course of time the castle passed from the Baldwin family to the Courtenays; an association which was to last for the next three and a half centuries. However, in 1537, one of the family who had become Marquis of Exeter was accused of conspiracy against the King. He was found guilty and beheaded, and Okehampton Castle was ordered to be dismantled. What is left is a series of broken walls, covering what were the moat and bailey, with a keep dominating the ruin.

The northern moor is a bleak, sometimes hostile place, a raised plateau of bog and windswept grass, with High Willhays topping 2,000 feet. Unfortunately, the area is crisscrossed with tracks laid down by the Services to reach their several firing ranges. On these it is possible to drive deep into the heart of the moor – but not without a twinge of conscience. This is really walking country and the car is an alien intrusion. To walk here in winter is to feel the character (and strength) of the moor. Underfoot it is like an immense peaty sponge; water is absorbed until the surface is a quaking mass of grass roots that one feels could at any moment give way.

The bitter 'heads down and hands in pockets' wind penetrates even the thickest clothing and a damp, all-enveloping mist can cover the almost featureless landscape in a matter of minutes. Under these conditions the moor is not to be trifled with and a good map, compass, stout boots and warm clothing are essential. You will probably be entirely alone, for the ponies and sheep will have drifted to the more sheltered perimeter where – with luck – fodder will have been provided by the commoners. If not, they must forage as best they can and compete throughout the winter for an ever-shrinking food supply.

A rule that I must admit to having frequently broken is not to go walking alone in bad weather – but if you do, at least let someone know where you are going. Most important of all, check whether the Services are using any of their ranges; if they are, red flags are flown around the area and on certain tors. Times of firing are also advertised in the local press and in post offices.

Lest I paint too dreary a picture of the high moor in winter, at other seasons it can be a delightful place with cottonwool clouds scudding across a blue sky, banks of heather on the hills and lacy ferns in the valleys. Many of the bogs dry out, and fresh, young grass appears – welcome feed for the sheep and ponies.

For the future, the threat to Dartmoor's unique character and atmosphere – it has been called 'The Last Wilderness in England' – is not only from Service use, mineral exploitation and reservoirs, but from the sheer number of visitors expected to descend upon the area in the next few years. It has been estimated that on a peak day in 1981 there will be no less than 95,000 people in the National

Park. This is a massive problem; moorland roads are unsuitable for heavy use by cars and coaches, and widening could destroy their character – particularly if the dry-stone walls were removed. Parking is another major problem.

The reconstituted Dartmoor National Parks Committee of the Devon County Council was appointed in August 1973 and consists of eighteen members – twelve appointed by the County Council and six nominated by the Secretary of State for the Environment. It has a number of functions, including overall planning control within the area. One of its first actions was to publish a very comprehensive Policy Plan which identified various parts of the moor as being most suitable for certain purposes. For example, the heart of both the north and south moor are regarded as 'Quiet Areas' where "the conservation of natural attractions is paramount". These areas will cater for "the non-motor borne visitors, particularly those who want to get away from noise, motor cars and other reminders of our urbanised society".

On the other hand, there are areas, such as Roborough Common, designated as 'Areas of More Intensive Use'. Facilities and large car parks could be constructed in such areas without detriment as there is already intensive recreational use.

However, it is worth remembering that elsewhere on the moor the National Parks Committee has been criticized, with some justification, for allowing the siting of large car parks capable of holding fifty cars or more on the skyline and visible for many miles, when there are numerous roadside hollows and disused quarries alongside moorland roads quite capable of absorbing vehicles four or five at a time with no visual intrusion. Instead of developing these spaces, many have, in fact, been 'banked' to prevent entry.

The Committee has recently experimented successfully with a 'Pony Express' minibus service carrying visitors on a tour of the more attractive side roads and encouraging them to leave their cars on the edge of the moor. They also run excellent Warden and Information Services based on a number of centres within the park. Leaflets are published on a variety of subjects, including fishing, riding and camping – a list can be obtained from the Dartmoor National Park Department, County Hall, Topsham Road, Exeter.

*Dartmoor ponies on Roborough Common, artful scroungers who have learnt to extract the last possible titbit from summer visitors – even though feeding is illegal because it encourages them to stray onto the roads. Perhaps they deserve all they can beg, for they often have a rough time in the winter.*

Another successful venture is a series of conducted walks starting from easily reached access points and covering a dozen or so different routes across the moor. The atmosphere is informal, the pace usually leisurely and the guides friendly and informative – an ideal way to enjoy the moor and to learn something of its history and character, all in congenial company.

As English a scene as you will find anywhere. Cricket on the lawn-like grass in front of Cockington Court. There are also delightful sunken gardens and lakes within the grounds.

CHAPTER FOUR

# TORBAY

STAND ON BERRY HEAD on a summer's day and Torbay stretches away before you in a great Mediterranean-blue crescent almost to the horizon. On a clear day the view will extend to Teignmouth and even as far as Portland Bill. There will be fishing boats in the foreground from Brixham, 'steamers' ferrying holidaymakers around the bay, and yachts by the score. The white wake of speedboats – like aircraft contrails – score figures of eight on the surface of the water. Whether one looks on Torbay as Queen of the South Devon Riviera, or the equivalent of all the Costas rolled into one, this is probably the most popular single holiday area in Britain.

Inland, a patchwork of fields, alternately red earth streaked with plough furrows and lush green grass, stretches away to the hills and tors of Dartmoor off on the horizon. Even the cattle are red – the famous South Devons. Look closely and you will also see the caravan and chalet camps catering for the annual influx of visitors; most hidden discreetly in folds in the gently rolling hills. Before leaving Berry Head walk around the defensive ramparts built during the Napoleonic Wars on top of the site of an Iron Age fort from which the promontory takes its name – 'Berry' from *burh*, the Celtic for 'fort'.

Torbay forms an excellent anchorage, with complete shelter from the south-westerly gales that are prevalent on this coast. Over the years it has sheltered an amazing variety of seafarers in a motley collection of craft – some welcome, many to be feared, or hated. In 1588 one of the finest ships of the Spanish Armada, the *Nostra Senora Del Rosario* – flagship of the Andalusian squadron – surrendered after colliding with another of the fleet and losing her

*109*

foremast. She was towed into the anchorage by the *Roebuck* (a privateer owned by Sir Walter Raleigh) and many of her crew imprisoned in the tithe barn of Torre Abbey which is still known as the Spanish Barn.

A score or so years later Moorish pirates were using the bay as a base from which to molest Channel shipping, apparently with complete impunity, for the Navy was being shamefully run down and the few ships left in service were deployed elsewhere. As if to rub salt in the wound, in 1667 De Ruyter mauled the Naval ships laid up in the Medway and then sailed down the coast to anchor in Torbay. He burned several local fishing boats and fired the odd cannon shot here and there, but fortunately did not test the almost non-existent shore defences.

Another Dutchman, William of Orange – Dutch Billy – landed at Brixham in 1688 with 15,000 men and 600 horses, *en route* to London and the eventual overthrow of King James. A statue stands rather forlornly on Brixham's Strand to commemorate the event.

During the eighteenth century, with England and France almost continuously at war, the anchorage in Torbay was used repeatedly by the Channel fleet. Admirals Hawke, Shovel, Rodney, Howe, St Vincent – and Nelson – all sheltered or assembled fleets here at one time or another. The long series of blockades and sea battles all contributed to the frustration of Napoleon's grand design and it was to Torbay that he was brought on the *Bellerophon* in July 1815 after his escape from Elba and surrender to the English fleet. He much admired the red cliffs and tree-lined hills, exclaiming "Enfin Voilà, Un Beau Pays", and compared these to Porto Ferrajo on Elba.

It seems that the local people, to whom he exhibited his customary magnetic charm, had mixed feelings about his presence. All were greatly curious, some sympathetic, and surprisingly few antagonistic. After forty-eight hours the *Bellerophon* was ordered around to Plymouth where another large crowd awaited his arrival – some say that more than a thousand boats were counted in the Sound. After eight days of indecision, during which time Napoleon even posed for a portrait, he was transferred to the *Northumberland* which carried him to St Helena and exile. So Torbay (and Plymouth) saw the final curtain fall on a long drama of revolution, aggression, conquest and dictatorship, and bade farewell to the man indirectly responsible for much of the expansion in the area. For during the Napoleonic Wars Torquay had grown from a small fishing village to a sizeable and fashionable resort.

Now, why should this growth have taken place so quickly at such an unlikely time? Many besides the ex-emperor had decided that this was indeed a beautiful place and with their favourite continental resorts closed because of the war, the 'nobility' flocked to Torquay for its scenery and mild climate. Also the great fleets of warships had often been detained in Torbay for months on end awaiting orders or suitable weather, and the officers had sent for their wives to join them. Houses, cottages and villas were built to cater for their needs.

By the mid-nineteenth century, the resort was well established

*The harbour at Paignton is tucked away at one end of the beach. It is small and dries out at low water, but has a useful launching slip for small boats; usually it also boasts a small fleet of self-drive runabouts. Altogether a pleasant place to sit and watch the comings and goings of boats, with the mellowed red sandstone buildings reflected in the still waters.*

*Nowadays, Goodrington is a part of Paignton and is rightly proud of its fine beach, boating pools and other 'family amusements'.*

and the South Devon Railway Company's line reached the town (or to be strictly accurate as far as Torre) on 15 December 1848. The line that brought in an ever-increasing number of visitors also carried out fish for the London market and the fishing fleet flourished. It was now becoming fashionable to live in the town as well as visiting it for holidays and on its pleasantly rounded hills sprung up the gleaming white Italian and Spanish-styled villas which have always contributed to the Mediterranean flavour.

In my younger days I remember that Torquay always stood very much on its dignity as the fashionable centre of the South Devon Riviera. Paignton, with its long sandy beach and pier, was for the family holidaymaker, while Goodrington – much more flippant – catered for 'day trippers' who flocked to the sea in their hundreds from the special trains which stopped within a few yards of the beach.

Not so many holidaymakers come by train nowadays, but the

*Paignton beach and pier, with the Festival Theatre off to the left. This is a fine stretch of reddish sand, backed by gardens and a promenade.*

vast numbers who arrive by car find entertainments to suit all tastes – from trips around the bay to opera at Paignton's Festival Hall, from cliff walks to stately homes and mansions. No doubt diligent search would also reveal the all-pervading bingo! Torquay, Paignton and Brixham were officially merged into the County Borough of Torbay in April 1968, but long before then their boundaries had expanded and become inextricably tangled.

I suppose it would be fitting to first visit the home of the oldest inhabitants; in fact, probably one of the first human dwellings in England – Kent's Cavern. The caves, only a mile from the centre of Torquay, were inhabited during the Stone Age and excavations down through the many layers of the stalagmite floor have revealed that mammoth, woolly rhinoceros, cave bear – and man – were all contemporary users of the extensive caves.

This important discovery, made possible largely through the

*One of the finest views in Torbay. The harbour and sea-front gardens at Torquay, seen from the Rock Walk. This is also a magnificent view at night for the harbour is floodlit and the zigzag paths of the Walk are lit with many different colours.*

efforts of William Pengelly, a nineteenth-century schoolteacher, mathematician and geologist, revealed that the advent of man was much earlier than had generally been believed. In 1859 Darwin published his *Origin of Species* and the discoveries at Kent's Cavern gave credence to the doctrine of evolution.

The caves today are well lit, the air is fresh and the temperature a comfortable and steady 52°F throughout the year. A guide conducts each party around the half mile or so circuit and, as guides are wont to do all over the world, points out the resemblance of individual stalagmites to people, places and objects.

Cockington village is not far away – the place that launched a thousand postcards. In spite of being one of the most photographed scenes in Britain and visited by thousands of visitors every year, this huddle of thatched cottages, complete with old forge, has managed to retain some of the original village atmosphere. Souvenirs, postcards and ice-cream counters are hidden discreetly behind cottage doors, whilst a rather self-consciously picturesque horse and carriage taxi-service carries visitors to and from the sea front.

Cockington Court, behind the village, is a gracious sixteenth-century manor house formerly owned by the Cary family and now the property of Torbay Council. The superb grounds are set with sunken lakes, woodland walks and formal gardens; when a game of cricket is in progress on the smooth lawns in front of the house the whole scene is almost too English to be true.

Torquay boasts with justification of its 'Walks' – from the steep, zigzag paths of the Rock Walk to the gentle stroll along the sea front, or through Torre Abbey Gardens. For the more energetic there is the up-hill down-dale walk along the Marine Drive, past Thatcher Rock to Hope's Nose which is always alive with sea

*If you drive around Marine Drive – and there can be few better ways of first taking in the atmosphere of Torquay – you will eventually come to Thatcher Rock, a haunt of sea-birds and a striking feature of the seascape.*

birds. Beyond, the cliffs stretch away past Anstey's cove (a popular spot in the summer) to Oddicombe and Maidencombe.

The inner harbour dries out at low tide leaving an assorted mixture of working and pleasure craft – mostly the latter these days – sitting on its sandy bottom. The local council once seriously considered the appalling sacrilege of filling in this centre-piece to provide more parking spaces. To its credit it changed its mind in time! On the hills around are the hotels, some still managing to maintain an aura of luxury and high-living, others converted to self-catering flats. Yet others have been demolished and luxury flats have arisen in their place.

I am always amused when travelling on the main road between Torquay and Paignton to pass a small gas-works hidden away in a hollow, apparently owned by neither resort and on neutral ground between. No doubt it is now disused, but it still gives the impression that neither party wants to identify this sordid piece of industrialization with its seafront.

As a complete contrast, within half a mile – on the Paignton side of the border – is Oldway House, a mansion of 115 rooms built in 1874 at a cost of more than £100,000 for the Singer family of sewing-machine fame. Paris Singer and his architect G. S. Bridgman were inspired in its design by the Palace of Versailles; it also has a touch of the Greek temples and it would not be out of place as the background for a Hollywood extravaganza.

It is usual to dismiss the house as a frivolity built by a man with more money than taste. This is too hard a judgement. The exterior is pleasing, with giant Corinthian and Ionic columns, the interior lavish in marble and gold – a mixture of many styles. The adjoining gardens, both formal and informal, are beautifully laid out and a pleasure to walk around. The house and grounds were purchased by the town for £45,000 in 1945, for which price they obviously received a bargain. Inside are council offices and a ballroom, etc., whilst the grounds contain tennis courts, bowling greens and a café.

As you drive between Paignton and Brixham you may glimpse, through gaps in the trees, a puff of white smoke and hear the nostalgic sound of a train whistle. Recovering from your astonishment, you will probably find yourself being paced by a steam

Oldway House, at Paignton, is often dismissed as an extravaganza built by a millionaire with more money than taste. This is too hard a judgement. It is an amiable, if eccentric, building with many interesting features, including the superbly laid-out gardens.

*A locomotive of the Dart Valley Railway, puffing smoke like a friendly dragon and with a tail of chocolate and cream coloured coaches, climbs a gradient on the line between Paignton and Kingswear.*

locomotive pulling several carriages, all in the old Great Western Railway livery of chocolate and cream. This is the Paignton to Kingswear line of the Dart Valley Railway which was opened in 1973.

The Dart Valley Railway Co., a commercially run organization assisted by volunteers, started a steam service from the old Buckfastleigh station to Totnes in 1969, seven years after the last British Rail train ran on the line. At the station they have static displays and workshops – a place to delight the hearts of small boys of all ages and both sexes. The two lines have proved very popular with visitors. More than 200,000 passenger journeys were made in 1975 and that figure has probably since been exceeded.

What an amazing human quality is nostalgia! Twenty years ago we all cursed steam trains as dirty, noisy air polluters, spraying soot indiscriminately over passengers, railways and track-side property alike. Diesels were so much quieter and cleaner, but they did break down more frequently. Now we have all discovered belatedly the romance of steam, the pleasure of rattling along in old carriages and the joy of exploring once derelict lines. With so many passengers a year travelling on the Dart Valley lines, there must be something in it all! One thing is certain, as photographic subject matter there is little to beat a steam locomotive pulling up a steep incline and belching clouds of evil smoke. Diesels just do not have the same character!

As one of the world's worst hoarders of inconsequential junk – "it *must* come in handy one day. . . !" – I have a great admiration for museum curators who can collect, date, catalogue and exhibit items of real value and make them all come alive to the public in general. Of course, all museums and exhibitions cater for the natural curiosity of the human race, particularly about things and events past. In fact, it has been postulated that the world will eventually come to an end not with a major conflict of nations, but with some curious individual saying "I wonder what this little red button does?" But I digress. I was about to mention Torbay Aircraft Museum a mile or so inland from Paignton front. This brings back nostalgic – if not pleasant – memories to anyone old enough to have tackled a spluttering incendiary bomb with sand and stirrup pump, or watched the contrails of dog-fights over the Devon skies with loser plunging into the blue waters of Torbay.

The scene is set by a Westland Whirlwind helicopter squatting like a giant grasshopper just inside the main entrance. Small boys – again of all ages and degrees of agility – scramble either through the gutted interior or up steps on the outside of the fuselage to reach the pilot's seat, there to give free rein to the imagination.

Indoor static displays of wartime equipment include aircraft instruments, parts of a fuselage dredged from the sea, an engine from the bottom of Torbay – not to forget wartime civilian ration books, tin hats and gas masks, etc. Outside, the Hurricane and ME 109 – these old adversaries – stand side by side on the grassy field.

*(Overleaf) The glorious sweep of Abbey Sands, one of Torquay's most popular beaches. In the background are Torre Abbey Gardens, beautifully laid out, impeccably maintained and always a riot of colour.*

Not wartime planes these, but full-scale replicas made for the film
'Battle of Britain' and authentic enough to pass as real from a distance.

Another unusual exhibit is the Rotorkite, a highly successful but
virtually unheard-of German 'secret weapon'. This ingenious
single-seat non-powered helicopter was winched from the deck of
a surfaced U-boat to enable the pilot to spot allied convoys up to
twenty-five miles away. As long as the submarine maintained a
steady speed of 10 miles an hour or so, the 'kite' could be flown to a
height of up to 400 feet.

'Modern' aircraft on display include a Vampire jet, Sea Venom
and a Gloster Meteor. But all is not of war; there are documents,
photos and relics of aviation as far back as 1909, including Bleriot's
first flight across the Channel and – twenty-five years later – the
Schneider Trophy Races.

Brixham has a salty tang – a no-nonsense workmanlike sort of
place, with houses peering over each other's shoulders as they
climb the steep hillsides around the harbour. Colourful too, with
the plaster of the houses echoing the bright colours of the fishing
boats moored below. Steep flights of well-worn stone steps connect narrow streets, their lack of width emphasized by the sheer
footage of yellow paint festooned along the edges.

Alas, in the summer Brixham very quickly reaches four-
wheeled saturation. With all car parks full, visitors are directed on
a tortuous one-way-route-of-no-return which eventually deposits
them, via many backstreets, on the outskirts of the town and heading back to Paignton. *En route*, if lucky, they catch a fleeting and
probably tantalizing glimpse of the crowded harbour.

For the down-at-pocket gourmet, the fish and chips in these
parts are excellent – and so they should be, in sight of the fish
quays. More exotic, and expensive, are the Brixham crabs and lob-
sters.

Originally Brixham started life as a Saxon settlement and
grew steadily around a creek inland of the present harbour. In 1525
John Leland described it as "a praty towne of fischar men called
Brixham", and fishing has always been the town's *raison d'être*. The
famous tan-sailed smacks have sailed out of Brixham harbour for
several centuries, using first hook and line, and later trawls. The

*A view of a war-time aerodrome? No, this is Torbay Aircraft Museum with a Hurricane and Messerschmitt 109 parked amicably together on the grass.*

fortunes of the fishing fleet have fluctuated over the years, with a decline at the end of the First World War, partly because the harbour dried out at low water. In 1916 a scheme was completed which extended the breakwater 3,000 feet out into the sea to provide an additional deep-water harbour.

Ironically, there was another decline after the Second World War, culminating in the reorganization of the industry on a co-operative basis and the building of new harbour installations and ice-making plant. Today fishing and tourism exist side by side and complement each other. Brixham has also been adopted by several artists and during the summer there is usually work exhibited on the quayside – in front of the scene that they must have painted thousands of times. A good place this to buy attractive paintings at reasonable prices for there are many styles on display and plenty of competition. A gallery close to the quay also contains a fine collection of paintings by local artists.

*(Above) William of Orange landed at Brixham in 1688, with 15,000 men and 600 horses, en route to London and the Crown. His statue stands on the quayside and is much appreciated by seagulls who rest on his head and small boys who sit on the base.*

*(Left) Brixham Harbour. Sturdy no-nonsense houses climb the hillsides, colour washed in every colour under the sun. The harbour is always jammed with an equally colourful mass of boats, working and pleasure. No wonder this is a favourite haunt of artists.*

When Brutus, grandson of the Trojan Aenas – the reputed colonizer of Britain – landed on these shores in 1170 B.C., he declaimed,

Here I sit and here I rest,
and this town shall be called Totnes.

A likely story? Well, maybe not, but it *was* repeated by Geoffrey of Monmouth who recorded the early history of Totnes and there *is* a granite block set in the pavement of Fore Street which has been called the Brutus Stone for as long as anyone can remember. Much more likely, however, is that this is a corruption of Bruiter's, or the Town Crier's, Stone. Discounting Brutus, the name of Totnes is thought to come from *tota*, a lookout, and *nes*, meaning a headland or hill.

To summarize the long history of this town, which incidentally claims to be one of the oldest boroughs in the country: coins were minted here between the reigns of Edgar and William Rufus, and the Saxons enclosed the town with earth ramparts upon which the Normans erected stone walls, some of which remain today. William the Conqueror granted a Norman knight, Judhael, the manor and it was he who built the castle on a high motte, with a bailey surrounding it.

From the top of the red sandstone keep with its massive 15-feet-thick walls there are superb views of the town and the River Dart in the valley below. The river has played an important role in Totnes's growth and the quays have been in use since Saxon times. In the fifteenth and sixteenth centuries wool and cloth were exported and the town grew rich – second only to Exeter in the wealth of its merchants. But it did not move with the times. The rest of Devon was dominated by the serge industry, but Totnes ignored this. Trade declined and the harbour gradually silted up.

One of the quays was used for many years by the 'steamers' operating from Dartmouth – recent victims alas of inflation, recession and the motor car. Now grass grows amongst the stone slabs of the quay where so many different types of craft have moored in their time. There is a touch of irony in the fact that one of the quayside buildings houses a Motor Museum, the mode of transport that has

*What a magnificent example of slate-hung house fronts! This is the Butter Walk at Totnes, where some of the houses date from the sixteenth century. Totnes has been very wise to prevent modern development spoiling the character of its main street. A historic town this, an important centre in Saxon times, later fortified by the Normans and a town of prosperous merchants in the Middle Ages.*

defeated so many others. 'Sic Transit Gloria Mundi', perhaps.

However, all may not be lost for recently barges have been using the river again, carrying, of all things, pumice from Italy. This is off-loaded from a ship at Dartmouth on to barges which in turn unload at Totnes. Why pumice? It seems this frothy form of lava is proving very suitable for the manufacture of certain insulated housing materials.

Totnes town is a place to savour slowly. No public-toilet-type bricks here or raw concrete, only mellowed stonework and matching-hued stucco. No chain store plastic shop fronts, or garish signs (well, hardly any), and even the small supermarkets are tucked discreetly away. Here is the essence of the small town, small friendly shops each dealing efficiently with its own commodity – furniture, books, vegetables, pictures, groceries – food for mind and body all readily to hand.

A place to browse and wander through with buildings on the same scale as the human beings who use them, not towering threateningly above in multi-storey profusion. Stroll under the overhanging top floor of the colonnaded Butter Walk – neither as old nor as impressive as Dartmouth's, but delightful all the same with its slate-fronted houses. Climb up a few steps to the Ramparts Walk and before long you will reach the 400-year-old Guildhall, built on a smaller scale than the rest of the town but none the worse for that. Open to the public, it contains amongst other items the town stocks in which four wrongdoers at a time might be incarcerated. Have a good look at the East Gate in Fore Street, with its fine old clock, and call in on the Elizabethan Museum close by. If you have time, also go for a stroll along the river bank – a pleasant spot particularly at high water.

By all accounts John Holland, Earl of Huntingdon and half-brother of Richard II, was a man of violent and impetuous temper. This involved him in two murders early in Richard's reign and there were no regrets when in 1386 he left on an expedition to Spain, led by John of Gaunt. When he returned two years later it was obvious that he would not be welcomed back in the capital. He was virtually exiled to the West Country – remote, it was hoped from the intrigues of the court – and he chose to settle at Dartington, near Totnes. Between 1388 and 1400 he built Dartington Hall on a grand scale with great hall, large quadrangle and many lesser rooms. He lived there until the deposition of Richard II, when he led an abortive uprising against his successor Henry IV, and was executed for his pains.

The Holland family, however, continued to live in the Hall for a further seventy-five years, but it was eventually forfeited to the

*The East Gate, with Gothic battlements and cupola, straddles Totnes's High Street. To the right, under the arch, steps lead up to the ramparts and thence to the old Guildhall.*

Crown after the discovery of a plot to overthrow Richard III. It came into the possession of the Champernowne family in the time of Elizabeth I and they were more fortunate, retaining the estate for more than 300 years and through eleven generations of the family.

Over the years the Hall fell into disrepair and when in 1925 two Americans, Dorothy and Leonard Elmhirst, bought it, the main buildings were in ruin. They needed the estate of 1,000 acres or so, and the buildings, for an ambitious experiment in the reconstruction of rural life. They wanted to bring back economic and social vitality to the countryside after the agricultural depression of the preceding years. A school was set up, allowing great freedom for each child to develop in its own way and offering education in the round – the co-ordination of work and play.

If that has a familiar ring as the formula for so many later disastrous experiments in "education through self-expression and freedom from discipline", all one can say is that it worked. Perhaps the Elmhirsts selected their pupils carefully, possibly the setting contributed, or maybe the time was just right for such an experiment. The whole plan was an adventure in ideas, and experiments in agriculture were carried on side by side with encouragement of all the Arts. It grew successfully as a place where education, industry and the arts could flourish together.

Today the Dartington Hall Trust administers a varied and complex organization, ranging from the manufacture of tweeds to the cutting and working of timber, and the production of fine glassware, not to mention running three farms and a building and contracting business – plus, of course, the school and many courses in all aspects of the Arts. In all this the original concept has not been lost.

The Hall and grounds are open to the public, subject to some obvious restrictions when parts are in use for activities. Have a look at the Great Hall – the centre of communal eating and entertainment in medieval days – with its 17-feet-long fireplace and replica hammerbeam roof (the original was removed in 1813, but the existing one is a faithful replica). The grounds are magnificent – particularly in springtime – with a row of Irish yew trees, known as the Twelve Apostles, adjoining a tournament ground

*Dartington Hall, near Totnes, was built by John Holland, Earl of Huntingdon, in the fourteenth century. Over the years, the building declined and when in 1925 it was purchased for a new venture, the structure was almost derelict. A trust was set up to administer the estate as an intellectual centre, with a sound practical background, and this has proved highly successful. This view shows the ancient tournament ground and the Irish yew trees known as the Twelve Apostles.*

terraced to provide seating for the original spectators. Nowadays just a pleasant place to sit, but no doubt in the past the scene of wild excitement. There are many fine and exotic shrubs – cherries, magnolias, camellias, rhododendrons, azaleas, etc. – with between them sculptures by Henry Moore and Soukep all in a perfect setting. You may well be tempted to buy at the Shinner's Bridge shop where the products of many of the activities are on display and for sale.

131

*Exeter's Guildhall is the oldest municipal hall and criminal court in the kingdom. The Tudor front, which was added in 1593, straddles the pavement of High Street.*

# CHAPTER FIVE

# EXETER (AND EXE TO TEIGN)

WHEN TRAVELLING BACK to the West Country by train from London or the north, it is at Exeter that I always notice a change in the pace of life – a sort of mental change of gear. The soft Devon burr of the station announcer and the civilized speed of presentation is a pleasant reminder that life is still not quite so hectic in this part of the world.

Perhaps the Roman legions marching down from the north in A.D. 50 also felt the need of a change of pace, for they penetrated little further into Devon and Cornwall. Having overrun the defences of the Celtic settlement Caerwisc, or 'the Camp by the River', they renamed the place Isca Dumnoniorum and set about rebuilding and administering it in their customary efficient manner. A high redstone wall was built around Isca and parts of it can still be seen in Rougemont Gardens, West Street and Southernhay.

The Romans stayed for 400 years until their authority ebbed and they were ousted by the local tribes and eventually replaced by the Saxons. They were predominantly an agricultural people and their conquest of the west was slow, probably achieved more by infiltration than outright conflict. Reaching the town in A.D. 700, they called it Exanceaster (from which the word 'Exeter' derives). The original settlement had grown into a sizeable centre for the surrounding area, but it was ravaged in A.D. 876 by the Danes – that scourge from the seas so feared by all within striking distance of the coast. They were driven out by King Alfred, but again in A.D. 1003 they attacked and plundered the town, eventually being forced back to the sea. Now belatedly, the defences were strengthened and it's clear that this was responsible for the transfer in 1050 of the diocese of Bishop Leofric from Crediton – which was undefendable – to the comparative safety of Exeter. As the Cathedral Foundation Charter states: "for pirates have been able to plunder the churches of Cornwall and Crediton – it has seemed clear that there is a safer defence against the enemies in the town of Exeter". This was an important stage in the town's development for under Leofric the foundations of the cathedral were laid and its importance as an ecclesiastical centre assured.

After the Battle of Hastings, William the Conqueror pursued the vanquished army of Harold into the West Country and Gytha, Harold's mother, sought sanctuary within the city walls. We are told that Exeter had about 460 houses at that time and a population of around 2,500 – and was the tenth largest town in England. William tried to take the city, but failed, and laid siege hoping to weaken the resistance of the inhabitants. In fact, it was he who weakened first, perhaps because there was news that Sweyn of Denmark was planning an attack in the east. Perhaps, too, he was influenced by the fact that Bishop Leofric had already declared for him. It seems that an 'honourable compromise' was reached. The citizens opened their gates and William, instead of putting all to the sword as was his wont, not only spared their lives but allowed them to keep their goods and confirmed their existing privileges. As he entered by the East Gate, unbeknown Gytha left by the West Gate!

William appointed Baldwin, a Norman Lord, as Seigneur and he constructed a castle on the volcanic outcrop called Rougemont. Little remains today of the Norman structure except for the gateway, castle yard and part of the red sandstone ramparts, but the gardens close by are a very pleasant place in which to stroll. About 1200, King John granted a series of charters conferring several rights, including that of electing a mayor. It seems likely, however, that these were confirmation of privileges already held from earlier kings and Exeter was, in fact, already an important market and port.

Exeter's importance in the affairs of the West Country meant involvement in all the wars, intrigues and skirmishes of the thirteenth, fourteenth and fifteenth centuries. For example, in the

*All that remains of Rougemont Castle is this Norman gate tower. Through the arch are the County Assize Courts. To the left, a doorway leads to Rougemont Gardens, a quiet tree-shaded spot with flower beds and walks, all on the slopes of the old moat.*

Prayer Book Rebellion of 1549, the city was besieged and when it finally gave in, the Vicar of St Thomas's was executed wearing his vestments and his body left hanging for nearly four years from the tower of his own church.

In Elizabethan times we find Exeter of paramount importance to the Queen. The city fitted out and manned three ships to sail against the Armada and for this was granted the motto on the city arms, 'Semper Fidelis'. The Devon sea-captains, so hated and dreaded by the Spanish, often met at Exeter. Drake, Raleigh, Hawkins, Frobisher and Gilbert are said to have used a first-floor room of Mol's Coffee House (now an art shop) for their meetings.

(Above) *A view that brings history alive. Drake, Raleigh, Hawkins and other sea-captains are believed to have used a first-floor room at Mol's Coffee House, on the left, to plan their expeditions.*

(Left) *The Ship Inn, in narrow St Martin's Lane, only a few yards from the coffee shop, is believed to have been another favourite haunt of Drake's.*

Another favourite haunt of Drake's was believed to be the Ship Inn in Martin's Lane which is still a popular inn today.

This short summary can do little more than scratch the surface of Exeter's history – so important a city deserves a whole book not just a short chapter. John Leland, who visited it in the 1530s, said: "The town of Excester is a good mile and more in Cumpace, and is right strongly waullid and mainteinid. Ther be diverse fair Towers in the Toun Waul bytwixt the South and the West Gate." When our old friend Daniel Defoe passed through it nearly two hundred years later it had grown considerably and he reported:

> From hence we came to Exeter, a city famous for two things which we seldom find united in the same town – viz, that it is full of gentry and good company, and yet full of trade and manufacturers also. The serge market held here every week is very well worth a strangers seeing, and next to the Briggs market at Leeds, in Yorkshire, is the gratest in England.

He went on, "They have the River Esk here, a very considerable river, and principal in the whole county; and within three miles, or thereabouts, it receives ships of any ordinary burthan, the port there being called Topsham."

Having a port at Topsham was not perhaps such an advantage as he was led to believe for in the reign of Henry III, the River Exe had been tidal to Exeter and small craft regularly came as far as the watergate. Then Isabella, Countess of Devon, built a weir across the river – to spite the Corporation, it is said – and the Earls of Devon followed her example by erecting other weirs downstream. They also built a quay at Topsham, the limit of navigation, and ensured that all goods landed there paid dues – to them!

The citizens brought lawsuits – and won them – but the Earls maintained their weirs. In 1539, the Corporation obtained an Act to enable them to improve the river, but in the event, exasperated by three hundred years of obstruction on the river, they eventually turned to a canal instead. They engaged John Trew of Glamorgan to survey a route from below Countess Weir to the city, where a quay would be built.

The 3,110 yards long canal was started in 1563 and completed two years later. It was only 3 feet deep and 16 feet wide, but could carry boats of up to 16 tons burthen and it had three locks – the first pound locks in Britain. Unfortunately, the entrance proved to be inaccessible at certain states of the tide and in 1675 it was carried a further half mile downstream and later in 1701 enlarged to 10 feet depth and 50 feet width, sufficient to take coastal craft of up to 150 tons.

*Exeter Canal, when it was built in 1563, had the first pound locks in Britain — that is, locks having sets of gates at both ends and allowing water to be raised or lowered in the chamber between. It was originally only sixteen feet wide, but has been much altered over the years, as the huge gates of Turf Lock, at the seaward end, testify.*

With the canal network spreading all over Britain and the possibility that Exeter could become the sea outlet for other West Country canals, it was again extended in 1825, this time a further two miles to Turf. Optimistically it was once more widened and a basin built at Exeter, with warehouses and other facilities. Traffic increased rapidly for a while, but the tide of events was against such an undertaking. Exeter's export of woollen goods had almost ceased and the coming of the Bristol and Exeter Railway in 1844 offered competition instead of collaboration. The coming of steamships, for which its dimensions were inadequate, also hastened the inevitable decline. Small tankers used the canal up until a few years ago, but commercial traffic has now virtually ceased. The building of the new M5 motorway bridge means that even

*The steam tug* St Canute *is one of the largest, and most popular, exhibits at the ISCA Maritime Museum centred on Exeter's old warehouses and quays. It is growing steadily with new craft being added every year.*

some pleasure craft will in future have difficulty in passing. For all that, the canal bank is a very pleasant place to walk, with extensive views across the estuary.

The old canal quays and warehouses at Exeter have taken on a new and very important lease of life. They now house the Maritime Museum, one of the city's most interesting present-day features. This is sponsored by the International Sailing Craft Association, ISCA – a most fortunate choice of initials for an organization operating in this historic Roman city. When Sir Alec Rose was rowed up the canal and into the basin to open the Museum on 27 June 1969 there were twenty-three craft on display; now there are more than sixty.

The aim of the Association is "to preserve actual craft and the gear that is used with them, and to accumulate knowledge of the history, evolution and use of the boats that are preserved".

Although devoted primarily to sailing craft, there are quite a number of other boats from all over the world that have been considered worth preserving. The steam tug, *St Canute* is not only one of the largest exhibits but also one of the most popular, particularly with youngsters who man the bridge and ring imaginary orders on the telegraph to the engine room far below. This is a much-travelled old lady for she was built in Denmark in 1931 and employed as a harbour tug at Odense until 1960. Then the Fowey Harbour Commissioners bought her and she was used in the estuary until 1968. ISCA acquired her shortly after.

The craft on display are really a cross-section of maritime history and range from a primitive Welsh coracle to a reed boat from Lake Titicaca, 12,000 feet up in the Andes. A Venetian gondola rubs shoulders with a pearling dhow which originated in Bahrain. There are outriggers, a dredger, an old lifeboat and a Bristol Channel pilot cutter. This is a museum to wander around, to clamber over, to look into and to touch. The whole place is alive, for other boats are being restored and there is the smell of pitch, the ring of hammers and the buzzing of saws.

Even the means of travelling from one part of the Museum to the other is almost a museum-piece in itself. One stands on a punt-like boat which is propelled by hand along a cable strung across the basin. The old warehouses should be thoroughly familiar to television viewers for they appeared in many different guises in the second series of the BBC's 'Onedin Line'. Props transformed them from the quays of Liverpool to seaports all over the world, and some most peculiar craft could be seen sailing the seven seas in the canal basin!

Inevitably, historically and in present-day terms, Devon's two cities, Exeter and Plymouth, must stand comparison. With a population of about 97,000 Exeter is much smaller than Plymouth with 250,000, but it has the overwhelming advantage of being more centrally placed as an administrative centre. It is at the hub of a communications network, with routes radiating like the spokes of a wheel. As we have seen, Exeter was an established Roman settlement when Plymouth was a huddle of mean dwellings on a muddy creek and it is this ease of communications that has led to its importance. Plymouth turned seawards and grew rich on the comings and goings of merchant ships and the Royal Navy, but its road communications have been difficult until very recent times. Exeter has a well-established international airport, while Plymouth has spent thirty years or so looking for a suitable site and now with good roads to Exeter the need has passed anyway.

Historically, there are other differences. Generally Plymouth has more often than not been 'Agin the King', whilst Exeter's loyalty to the Crown seems to have been unswerving. Well almost – it's true that during the Wars of the Roses she changed sides, but eventually came down firmly for Edward IV, who gave the mayor his sword as a mark of favour.

Plymouth never seems to be quite sure whether it is a holiday resort (with a small 'r') as well as the 'Centre of 100 Tours'. Visitors are welcomed rather self-consciously – and at a minimum cost to the rates. However, all this could change. Plymouth City Council has recently appointed a Director of Tourism and Marketing with a brief to set up a marketing bureau and to get a larger share of the tourism market. Plymouth also has its eye on the lucrative conference and convention trade.

Exeter has no illusions – it is definitely not a holiday resort. Not that visitors are unwelcome – far from it – it is just that it stands very much on its dignity as a cathedral and university city, and the centre of local government for the county. Little attempt is made to divert the thundering hordes from the M5 as it skirts the city. There are few multi-storey car parks to tempt the casual visitor and even its fiendishly complicated one-way traffic system seems designed to decant motorists as painlessly as possible on the outskirts of the city – on the other side!

In June 1975 Exeter's High Street was 'pedestrianized' (it makes one wince to use such a word, but at least it is descriptive). Cars were banned, but buses have been allowed to continue moving freely through the area and to stop for passengers. There have been grumbles that a pedestrian still cannot walk at ease without continually casting an eye over his shoulder. Nevertheless, on the whole the experiment has been a success and the restrictions are to be made permanent. To stop buses using the street would involve expensive rerouting and this will have to await the outcome of Exeter's Transportation Study, at present on the stocks.

*Exeter's High Street, modern yet dignified. The red brick so extensively used in re-building blends well with the old red sandstone walls.*

Exeter has also tried an experimental 'Park and Ride' scheme for a limited period – with some success. These expedients will become more and more common in our cities as time goes by, making the centres much more pleasant places in which to walk. Plymouth is also toying with such a scheme.

One of the attractions of Exeter is that architecturally it has the delightfully haphazard, almost casual, air of a city that has grown over the centuries with little attempt to impose any overall plan. Very early on, it exhausted all space within the old town walls and the houses spilled down the slopes to the river and beyond. A fine hotch-potch of styles, periods and materials, with the cathedral rising gloriously above it all.

Hitler's bombers flattened Plymouth; at Exeter they were more

*One of Exeter's delightfully secluded pedestrian shopping ways. Warm and welcoming in style, with no risk to life or limb from passing vehicles, these are deservedly popular with shoppers.*

selective. Plymouth started rebuilding with a clean sheet and the 'grand design' is orderly and geometrically pleasing, but with a certain coldness. Exeter opted for red brick and the centre has a warmer, more intimate feeling, with small enclosed pedestrian shopping precincts and sunken gardens. It is the unexpected that makes a walk through Exeter's streets so exciting — a sudden glimpse of the cathedral tower through a narrow alleyway, a view of the old city walls, a mellow red sandstone church suddenly coming into view around a corner, a road that ends abruptly in cobbled steps, the distant sparkle of water in the canal basin, or even the fine panoramic view from Rougemont Gardens so close to the city centre. One could almost fall down one of the most un-usual features. These are the steps in Princesshay leading down to the underground passages. Cut through solid rock in medieval

*Cobbled Stepcote Hill, terminating in St Mary Steps, is believed to have been the medieval 'main road' west out of the town.*

*St Mary's Steps Church has a famous clock with figures that strike the hours. It is said that they represent Henry VIII and two soldiers with javelins, but they are also known as Matthew Miller and his sons. The time-scarred timber on the left is part of 'The House that Moved'. For more than 600 years this fine old house stood in Frog Street, but then it proved to be in the way of a new road. With infinite care it was moved bodily 75 yards to its present position. An eminently practical and sensible solution.*

times — some say Roman, but there's no proof of this — these narrow passages carried fresh water from springs in the Longbrook Valley into the centre of the city. At points along the way buckets could be lowered through the roof to scoop up the water. Originally, this flowed through the natural rock, or in a wood-lined channel, but in 1420 it was diverted into a 3-inch lead pipe and terminated in a public fountain. As the Guide says, it is a unique experience to ease one's way through these narrow slits of tunnels barely wide enough for one person.

Exeter has taken care to preserve a fine collection of old buildings of all periods of its history. The Guildhall is, to quote the plaque on its walls: "The Oldest Municipal Hall and Criminal Court in the Kingdom. Rebuilt in 1330 on Norman and possibly Saxon foundations." The arched Tudor front was built in 1593 and straddles the pavement of High Street. Inside, there is some fine oak panelling, each panel having a different carving.

Incomparably the finest building in Exeter is, of course the cathedral. How does one do justice to such a building? No words can really describe the splendour of the interior. Looking down the nave as one enters, the Purbeck marble columns stretch away to the quire, like the trunks of a petrified forest. The superb vaulting continues the analogy for this is like the delicate tracery of branches and is, incidentally, the longest unbroken stretch of Gothic vaulting in the world.

There is evidence to suggest that there was a monastery hereabouts as early as 670. Certainly in 932 a minster was built for use by the monks, but this was destroyed in 1003 by the marauding Danes. In 1050, Leofric was enthroned as the first Bishop of the See of Exeter (his effigy is in the Lady Chapel). The original small church was not grand enough for the Normans and between 1112 and 1137 Bishop William Warelwast built a cathedral next to the minster. This lasted for little more than a hundred years, but the two great towers remain today, incorporated into the present cathedral and looking rather like castle keeps. A few other pieces of Norman masonry also remain, notably the buttresses outside the north wall of the nave, but there are few clues to the size and shape of this building.

The building as we see it today has grown over the centuries,

*The West Front of Exeter Cathedral, the base of which consists of niches, each filled with a statue. Above is a magnificent window with decorated stone tracery. The two great Norman towers on each side of the building were incorporated in the thirteenth century.*

each bishop adding, enriching and decorating. Bishop Bronescombe built the Lady Chapel and after his death in 1280, Bishop Quivil erected the magnificent arches that exist today – and then knocked down the inner walls of the Norman towers to make the interior more spacious. Next came Bishop Bytton, who added the four eastern bays of the quire in 1300. The arcade and gallery were built during the next few years.

In 1342, work commenced on the west front and the minstrels' gallery was added. By 1369 the vaulting of the five western bays of the nave had been completed and the cathedral was much as we see it today. It seems to have continued serenely until the Reformation when it suffered much damage – the original magnificent reredos was mutilated and many of the tombs and statues were defaced. When Cromwell occupied the city more damage was done, and during the Commonwealth, church prayer book services were banned. With complete insensitivity a huge wall of bricks was built on top of the screen, effectively dividing the cathedral into two churches, the one in front of the screen being used by the Presbyterians whilst that beyond was occupied by the Independents (later to become Congregationalists). Fortunately, during the reign of Charles II this eyesore was torn down and much done to restore the cathedral to its former glory.

The bishop's throne is a superb example of local materials – Devon oak fashioned by Devon craftsmen. Elaborately carved and more than sixty feet high, it was built in 1312 to the order of Bishop Stapledon. Almost unbelievably the whole structure was put together without the use of a single nail, only wooden pegs being used to secure the joints. This saved it from the reforming zeal of the Cromwellian era for it was quickly taken apart and hidden before any troops entered the building.

It may well have also saved it from damage in the last war, for the throne, together with the fourteenth-century glass in the east window, was taken down and stored in a safe place. The cathedral was bombed in May 1942 and considerable damage caused, particularly to St James's Chapel where screens and windows were smashed. With exquisite care and craftsmanship all the damage was repaired soon after the war and new stone has now mellowed to match the old.

Another feature that must not be missed is the very fine fifteenth-century astronomical clock with Latin inscription meaning, "the hours perish and are reckoned to our account". Also the minstrels' gallery up on the north side of the nave – and the choir screen, with three pointed Purbeck marble arches and seventeenth-century painted panels. Do look closely too at some of the very fine wood carving, not just the elaborate pieces but also down to the rather quaint little misericords in the quire. If you can, go into the chapter house and see Ken Carter's striking figures depicting creation from Genesis to the Resurrection. In contemporary style, these are not everyone's cup of tea, but like them or not, they

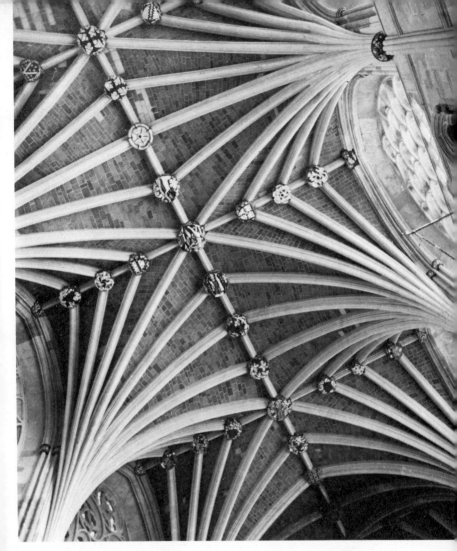

(Above) *Close-up of the nave roof showing the tracery of the vaulting, decorated at each intersection with superbly colourful bosses. The delicate-looking arrangement, incidentally, supports more than 5,000 tons of stone. The old-time architects had few theoretical means of checking their designs, but they were seldom wrong!*

(Left) *This is the triumphantly effective view with which you are confronted on entering the West Door. The nave stretches away into the distance, Purbeck marble columns looking like trunks of a petrified forest. The roof represents the longest unbroken expanse of Gothic vaulting in the world.*

(Above) *The astronomical clock in Exeter Cathedral.*

(Right) *The small wood carvings in the cathedral are of as much interest as the larger and more monumental works. It is obvious that this delightful little elephant — on the underside of a seat — was not taken from life. The carver had clearly never seen one and worked from the best description available.*

certainly cannot be ignored. Outside is the Close, a pleasant tree-shaded expanse of lawn where you can sit and plan the next excursion – or just laze and watch Exeter's life flow gently by.

To the north of the city is the University which has evolved slowly from a School of Art established in 1855. Buildings, facilities and disciplines have been added over the years and in 1955 it attained full university status with the right to award degrees. The campus is superbly situated and covers some 320 acres with mature trees and gardens (including an arboretum) and fine views across the Exe estuary.

In 1967 the Northcott Theatre was built as part of the complex. This was – and still is – a most exciting venture, for the West Country is not noted for enthusiastic patronage of the professional theatre. Many another such enterprise has foundered on the rocks of public apathy. Not so the Northcott; it has proved highly successful in presenting a wide range of entertainment, from ballet to music hall, poetry readings to pantomime.

Dawlish, ten miles or so from Exeter, takes its Saxon name from the small stream, known locally as The Brook, which nowadays makes a leisurely way down through the Lawn Gardens, over a series of low weirs and through man-made pools to the sea. A perfect setting for the swans and wild fowl that give life to the scene, with their brightly inquisitive comings and goings.

From a Saxon settlement it grew into a small fishing village and then, rather like Torquay, benefited from an influx of 'visitors of quality' unable to travel abroad to their favourite resorts because of the Napoleonic Wars. The Strand, at that time just a huddle of huts by the waterside, was rebuilt as shops, and other houses were built on the hillsides to cater for the visitors. A *Guide to Watering Places* published in 1815 has this to say of the resort: "Dawlish – is generally esteemed equally salutary for invalides with that of Montpellier, or Nice and therefore, it is frequently prescribed for persons labouring under pulmonic disorders, and all the long train of complaints known under the vulgar name of declines." How our forefathers did cherish their ailments!

The railway came in 1846 – straight along the seafront for no other route was possible. Brunel carried his line across the valley on a low granite viaduct, but left access to the beach through an arch. This was part of Brunel's famous Atmospheric Railway system – a daring experiment that deserved to succeed, but failed for a most unusual reason. Why? Well, the system employed compressed air with pumping stations every few miles to supply the motive power – ten, in fact between Exeter and Totnes. A plunger underneath the train was sealed in a metal pipe on the track, with a slot allowing access for the connecting rod. As pressure of air built up behind, the train was propelled forward at speeds of up to 68 m.p.h. All very ingenious and extremely quiet in operation – while it worked! Unfortunately, the slot had to be sealed with leather, and rats ate this, causing continuous trouble. Also the leather became hard through the action of the weather and lost its essential pliability.

Eventually the experiment was abandoned after more than £400,000 of the South Devon Railway Company's money had

*The railway runs straight along the front at Dawlish, but this in no way detracts from the charms of this resort, with its long sandy beaches and colourful gardens.*

*I wonder why someone does not publicize this as one of the most scenically satisfying stretches of railway line in Britain. Between Dawlish Warren and Teignmouth the train pops in and out of tunnels, past fantastically eroded cliffs, and then races along only feet from the breaking waves.*

been wasted. Brunel's reputation was, however, sufficiently great for him to survive this setback and to move on to other more successful schemes. All that remains today is a large squat brick tower at Starcross – sole survivor of the pumping stations. This is a superbly beautiful line with the train diving into red sandstone tunnels, emerging to race along embankments only feet from the breaking waves, past sun-spangled estuaries and the deer park of Powderham Castle. If British Rail knew what they were about they would advertise this as *the* scenic trip of Britain!

Dawlish Warren is a large spit of land facing Exmouth across the mouth of the Exe estuary. Most of the spit is actually sand, and winter storms were playing havoc with it – in fact, there were fears that the Warren would eventually be washed away completely. A coastal protection scheme using huge stone blocks appears to have secured it from seawards and grass-planting should help to prevent erosion of the dunes, but as on so many other popular strips of coast, one of the problems is the sheer number of people trampling across the dunes and literally wearing them away.

It is said that the dunes are haunted by the ghosts of the crew of the *Zeuse*, a Dutch privateer from Flushing which attacked Exmouth in 1782. She was soundly beaten and sunk by the *Defiance*, and the Dutch dead were buried on the Warren. Be that as it may, no self-respecting ghost would attempt to haunt there today, at least not during the summer months, when the dunes vibrate with the din from roundabouts, bingo halls, betting shops, candy-floss stalls, go-karts and all the paraphernalia of a 'popular beach'. But walk a few hundred yards in either direction and the atmosphere changes completely – towards Teignmouth there is a pleasant sea walk which follows the railway by red sandstone cliffs.

In the other direction there is a mile or so of soft fine sand – sand to tickle the toes of young children, to get in the sandwiches and tea cups carried precariously from the cafe nearby, sand on which to rest grandma's and grandad's deckchairs, for dad and the kids to burrow into, making moats and sculptured castles of fantastic design – all, alas, to disappear under the ever-encroaching waves as the tide comes in and wipes the slate clean for tomorrow's visitors to start all over again.

But one of the main features of this stretch of coast is the superb red cliffs, eroded into fantastic shapes by wind and waves. Between Teignmouth and Dawlish are two large rocks standing out to sea and known as 'The Parson and Clerk'. The story goes that many years ago the Bishop of Exeter was taken ill while staying in Dawlish. A certain ambitious parson from a nearby town made a habit of coming to visit him – not through charitable thoughts, but because he was after the bishop's job. One wild night he heard that the old man had taken a turn for the worse and not wasting a moment set off with his clerk, both on horseback, for Dawlish.

In the pitch black, gusty weather they lost their way and were

*Teignmouth is typical of many Devon beaches. The red-tinged sand is attractive, and the sandstone bulk of the Ness forms an ideal backdrop.*

relieved when eventually out of the gloom appeared a figure. He offered to lead them to Dawlish not far away, but suggested that first they might like to come to his humble dwelling and refresh themselves. They agreed and on going inside found a number of wild-looking locals drinking ale. After a good meal – and many drinks – they joined in the roistering and singing. So they passed the night and completely forgot the purpose of their journey.

In the morning a messenger arrived and announced in sepulchral tones to the bemused company: "The Bishop of Exeter is dead." The parson and clerk dashed in panic to their horses, but both refused to move. They looked around and found that their drinking companions had turned into a crowd of demons. But worse was to come, for the cliff top had been transported out to sea and now the waves were breaking all around them! The parson and his clerk were never heard of again, but next morning local fishermen found two new red sandstone rocks off the shore – and there was something very familiar about their shape!

Just down the coast is Teignmouth, a resort, but not one that dies of boredom in the winter months. The town has a self-contained social and commercial life, with a pleasantly compact shopping centre. It also has docks, most of which were built in 1821 by George Templer of Stover to ship granite from his Haytor quarries on Dartmoor. The quays are used nowadays for the export of china clay – ball clay from the Bovey basin, near Newton Abbot – but a shifting sand bar at the mouth of the estuary makes navigation difficult for large ships.

There is also a tradition of ship-building and fishing here and the port was important enough to be sacked by the French in 1690. It was bombed too in the Second World War when 'tip and run' raiders hit the area. As a resort it became fashionable in the late eighteenth and early nineteenth centuries and much of the architecture dates from this time. Keats stayed here and liked the place, writing:

> Over the hill and over the dale,
> And over the bourne to Dawlish,
> Where Ginger-bread wives have scanty sale,
> And Ginger-bread nuts are smallish.

Teignmouth front is a nice mixture of the brash and the genteel. Trips around the bay, winkles on the pier, deckchairs in the sun and the Salvation Army on Sunday. Behind the Promenade is the Den, six acres or so of green lawn laid out with flower beds and shelters; in front an excellent beach of fine red sand.

Facing Teignmouth across the river is the Ness, a mighty sandstone headland dominating the entrance to the estuary, with Shaldon in its shadow. Catch the ferry across (or walk over the bridge a little further inland) and climb the headland for a magnificent view of the whole estuary and surrounding countryside.

Shaldon has a modest elegance, mainly from its small but striking Regency houses, a delightful jumble of styles and colours nicely set off by narrow streets, pocket-handkerchief-sized gardens and more than its fair share of palm trees. There is a tunnel under the Ness headland, once used by smugglers, of course, and leading to Ness Cove, a delightfully secluded spot.

*It is interesting to see the Dutch influence on houses at Topsham.*

# CHAPTER SIX

# EAST DEVON

---

THE COASTAL LIMITS of East Devon are easy to define – the Exe estuary and Exmouth at one end, Seaton and the Dorset county boundary at the other. Inland, the area is more difficult to pin down, but let us follow the River Exe to Tiverton and then cut across to the Black Down Hills, shared by both Devon and Dorset. I will apologize in advance to anyone left on the wrong side of this arbitrary line and merely say in defence that the District Council boundary is even more elastic, for administratively this stretches almost to the foothills of Exmoor.

The characteristic inland scenery of gently rolling hills, rich farmland, remote hamlets and scattered villages differs little from the pattern set elsewhere in Devon, but the coastal strip has a different feeling to that south of the Exe. Perhaps it is the abruptly 'sawn-off' appearance of the sandstone and chalk cliffs, or the long pebble-ridge beaches, . . . or even the mellowness of the seaside towns and villages.

Let us look first at Topsham, mentioned in an earlier chapter for its importance as Exeter's port when the Exe was closed by a weir. Nowadays it is virtually a suburb of Exeter, but for all that it has managed to retain a very distinct and separate identity. The quays have long since silted up, but its busy past is remembered in the names of the old inns – the Steam Packet, the Lighter, Passage House Inn and the Lord Nelson.

The houses are in a rich mixture of styles and surprisingly the most popular is Dutch. In fact, as you walk down the street you could be in almost any Dutch seaside town. The delightful small courtyards and alleyways also reflect the influence. Why should this be? Well, many of the houses were built from bricks brought back as ballast on ships returning from Amsterdam and thereabouts. No doubt the sea-captains trading regularly along the Dutch coast also liked what they saw and built accordingly.

Topsham grew on the export of Devonshire serge and almost died when the woollen industry collapsed towards the end of the eighteenth century. Luckily, its ship-building industry flourished, together with all the ancillary activities – rope and chain manufacture, etc. – and these carried it on until well into the nineteenth century. Today it is quiet, but not decayed, for there are many small-boat moorings on the river's edge. A modern block of flats – not as hideous as many, but as out of place as most – occupies a choice site by the banks of the Exe.

Five miles downriver is Exmouth. If I were asked to say why Exmouth is different from so many other coastal towns I would plump for its layout. It divides into three distinct entities – the town, the seafront and the docks. The small hamlet that existed in 1001 was burnt to the ground by a party of marauding Danes sailing their longships up the Exe estuary. It was rebuilt and grew gradually as a port, but even as late as the eighteenth century was still being troubled by pirates from Tunis and Algeria.

By the mid-nineteenth century it was a thriving harbour where ships of 500 tons or more were unloaded and their cargoes transported by 'lumpers', who took their barges upriver to Topsham and Exeter. Their loads included hides pickled in salt, guano, timber, grain and salted cod from the Newfoundland Banks. As at Topsham, ships of all types and sizes were built and the ancillary trades flourished – rope and spar-making, sailmaking, etc. With the coming of steam and larger ships the port declined, although large landings of fish, herrings in particular, were made until about 1920 when the general depression in the fishing industry brought a sharp decline. Today the docks are still used, but on a diminished scale: coasters land grain, timber, coal, fertilizer, etc., and a few fishing boats bring in their catches. Around the dock area and bordering the river is an unusual sort of shanty town of holiday homes. One day no doubt some planning authority will cast a jaundiced eye over the area and the lot will be bulldozed into the sea – and much of the character of the area will disappear for ever!

*Just like a dolls' house, on a much larger scale. 'A La Ronde' is a cottage orné, built by the Misses Jane and Mary Parminster, ardent collectors of shells. They used these to decorate a gallery on the upper floor.*

Exmouth town has nothing very inspiring in the way of architecture, but just outside the town are two interesting oddities, or cottages *ornés*. 'A La Ronde' was built by the Misses Jane and Mary Parminster in 1798 and is a copy of San Vitale at Ravenna. It is an almost circular building (actually there are sixteen flat sides) of two storeys, with square and diamond-shaped windows of differing sizes surmounted by a tiled roof containing a series of dormer windows. To cap it all there are tall brick chimneys and a balcony! There is a slight air of fantasy about the whole place – it could almost be a very large doll's house – and perhaps this is not surprising because the good ladies were indefatigable travellers and collectors of curiosities (including dolls). They also collected prints, engravings, samplers, feathers – and shells in their thousands. Why shells? Because they were used to decorate a gallery on the upper floor. This is a most unusual feature with the shells arranged in ornate and fanciful designs around stairs and walls. The house is frequently open to the public during the summer months, and worth a visit. Just down the road, but not quite so well known, is 'Point-in-View'. This is a tiny chapel also built by the Misses Parminster, with alms-houses adjoining for "four spinsters over fifty years of age and approved character". The unusual name is said to derive from the motto over the entrance to the chapel; "Some point in view – We all pursue".

Exmouth's main claim to fame must be its two-mile-long stretch of sandy beach, barely broken by the red sandstone bulk of Orcombe Rocks off at the eastern end. The Esplanade and Marine Drive run alongside the beach, separated only by pavement and low wall. Perhaps the only criticism is that it lacks a central focal point – Torquay has its inner harbour, Paignton its Festival Theatre, Teignmouth its pier – all that Exmouth can manage is a café or two, a small park and a few rather half-hearted children's amusements. However, one cannot have everything, the beach is superb, the bathing good at most states of the tide, and the walk over the cliffs to Littleham Cove is magnificent. Take a good look at the beach for you will see precious little more of sand as far as the Dorset border.

From here on up the coast is Raleigh country, although his name is seldom associated with East Devon in the same way that Drake's dominates the history of South Devon. We all know the legend of the cloak laid at Elizabeth's feet, yet this great Englishman and colonizer never seems to have caught the public imagination like his contemporary. He too sought to expand England's influence and to curb the worldwide power of Spain, albeit with due benefit to his own pocket at the same time.

Raleigh was a man of many parts, a jack of all trades – explorer, soldier, sailor, courtier, poet, writer, historian and, on the face of it, he was successful at all of them. Yet ironically, few of his ventures endured, and tragically he died a traitor's death in the Tower of London. He was a man of his times – adventurous, courageous, ambitious, sometimes cruel, impatient, ready to risk all on the out-come of a voyage of exploration, or semi-legal privateering.

Born in 1552, or thereabouts, at Hayes Barton, a cobb and thatch farmhouse not far from East Budleigh, the boy grew up in quiet, gentle surroundings, a far cry from the places he was to visit later in his life. Millais's famous painting of two youngsters listening raptly to an old sailor's yarn shows the pebble beach at Budleigh Salterton and the two boys were Walter Raleigh and his half-brother Humphrey Gilbert. His father sent him to Oxford to study, but in 1569 he left to seek adventure and fought on the Huguenot side in the French religious wars. His first sea-command came about twelve years later, in the *Falcon*, a ship of 100 or so tons owned by the Queen and forming part of a flotilla of seven led by Humphrey Gilbert.

*Marine Drive, which runs beside Exmouth's two-mile-long sandy beach, comes to an end at Orcombe Point. It's worth continuing on foot around the rocks, or over the headland, to reach Sandy Bay the other side.*

*Raleigh was born in this cobb and thatch farmhouse, Hayes Barton, near East Budleigh. His father did not own the farm, but leased it from the Duke family at nearby Otterton. It is obvious that the place had happy associations for Raleigh, for later in life he tried, unsuccessfully, to buy the house.*

Later, spoiling for action, he went to Ireland, with the rank of captain and in charge of a hundred men to fight a Spanish and Italian force which had landed to assist the rebels. Returning from Ireland in 1581 with Lord Grey's despatches he was questioned by the Privy Council about the progress of the campaign. With his background knowledge and original ideas for solving the problems of this troubled country he soon had the ear of the Queen.

From then on his rise in favour was meteoric. The ageing monarch obviously found this handsome and gallant six-footer – soldier, adventurer and poet – attractive and interesting. Soon he was receiving sinecures and appointments from the Queen. As a courtier he excelled, wearing extravagant clothes and buying expensive jewels, but for all his polish he still retained his broad Devon accent.

With some of his new-found wealth he organized and equipped an expedition to the Americas. This was successful and his star continued to ascend. He became a Member of Parliament, his fortune grew, and on 6 January 1585 he was knighted by the Queen.

Other successful expeditions to the New World followed, including those that brought back the potato and possibly tobacco, although it seems likely that Sir John Hawkins first introduced the latter into England.

It is not clear how many ships Raleigh contributed to the fleet that defeated the Armada, but he certainly provided the flagship. Built to his own design she was first called the *Ark Ralegh* but later sold to the Crown and renamed the *Ark Royal* – the first of an illustrious line of that name. She was a superb ship and the Lord Admiral, Howard of Effingham, was delighted with her. But now there were rumblings at Court. As Raleigh had originally ousted Leicester from favour so a new favourite was emerging in the Queen's eyes. The second Earl of Essex was what Raleigh had been ten years earlier – tall, handsome, courageous, proud and courteous – he was also of gentle birth which gave him an advantage over Raleigh. The Queen was adept at playing off her favourites one against the other and there is little doubt that from this point some of Raleigh's influence declined.

Then suddenly in 1592 he was disgraced, dismissed from the Court and imprisoned in the Tower. The cause of his downfall – Elizabeth Throckmorton (later to become his wife) – was imprisoned there at the same time. News of his affair with a lady of the Privy Chamber had reached the ears of the Queen and, like a later monarch, she was not amused. Her favourites were expected to be true to her alone. Raleigh had played with fire, apparently believing – quite wrongly – that his position at Court was unassailable.

Although imprisoned in the Tower – in comparative comfort –

*Raleigh's father was a churchwarden at East Budleigh church and the family pew was here. All the bench ends are superbly carved and represent a variety of subjects. On the left is the Raleigh coat of arms, on the right a fine representation of a bearded figure.*

his ships continued their expeditions and privateering. One of them captured the *Madre de Dios*, probably the richest single prize ever to be taken, and she was brought into Dartmouth. But soon the cargo started to disappear, pilfering was rife, and the Queen became concerned about the Crown's share of the booty. This was a fortunate turn of events for Raleigh, for he was released from the Tower to restore some order and to safeguard the Queen's treasure.

However, he was never again to fully regain the Queen's confidence – his enemies made sure of that. During the closing years of Elizabeth's reign they ranged against him. Lord Cecil in particular worked to undermine his position and when James came to the throne he disliked almost everything about Raleigh. They were opposites in character, appearance, manners and beliefs. James had plans to make peace with Spain and Raleigh was one of the most feared and hated enemies of that country. He stood in the way and he had to be sacrificed. In July 1603 he was arrested on an obviously trumped-up charge and taken back to the Tower. The charge, almost unbelievably, was one of plotting with the Spanish (his sworn enemies) to overthrow King James.

Raleigh defended himself vigorously, but the outcome was foregone – the Privy Council and King had already determined his guilt and he was condemned to death. Literally within sight of the scaffold he was reprieved and lodged in the Bloody Tower. He was to spend thirteen long years here and passed the time writing his *History of the World*, a tremendous undertaking. Prince Henry, James's son, said, "No one but my father would keep such a bird in a cage." Raleigh fretted for action and eventually he was released to lead a further expedition to Guiana, in search of the elusive El Dorado, but only after he had given an undertaking not to molest the Spaniards. He kept *his* word but when his ships reached the mouth of the Orinoco river he was taken ill and entrusted one of his commanders – Laurance Keymis – with the task of investigating the nearby gold mines. He disobeyed instructions and became involved in an affray between English and Spanish. Raleigh's son, Wat, was killed and the whole affair became a fiasco.

News travelled ahead and when Raleigh arrived back at Plymouth on 21 June 1618, a sick and tired man, he was met by Sir

Lewis Stukely who had a warrant for his arrest. This time there was to be no reprieve. Further plots and conspiracies were 'discovered', old charges revived, and the result was a foregone conclusion. On a cold winter's morning – 28 October 1618 – he was beheaded on a block especially erected in Palace Yard, Westminster.

Quite apart from its associations with Raleigh, Budleigh Salterton is an attractive little seaside town. Its name derives from the salterns, or salt-pans, in which seawater was evaporated by monks in the thirteenth century. The A376, always crowded during the summer months, goes straight through, past the twenty or so shops, then dips down to the pebble beach, only to do a steep climb up the other side and a sharp left turn at the top. If you can park your car this is the spot to see the pebble beach stretching away for several miles in each direction. On the beach there is all the paraphernalia of fishermen – pots, nets and ropes – with usually a boat or two hauled high by windlass and cable.

Broadly speaking, Ottery St Mary is also in Raleigh country, although there are no direct links with the family. In fact, the most famous son of this small town is Samuel Taylor Coleridge, the poet and philosopher. Its best-known feature is the massive parish church of St Mary set on a hillside above the town. From the outside it is obvious that this is no ordinary small-town church and as you enter the door you realize that it is magnificent – like a miniature cathedral. This is no accident for if you have already visited Exeter Cathedral you will immediately notice a certain resemblance. When the church was rebuilt and enlarged by Bishop Grandison in the fourteenth century it was closely modelled on the cathedral – on a smaller scale – with two transeptal towers, chancel and Lady Chapel beyond. There is even a wooden clock, very much like the one at Exeter. The colourful bosses of the vaulted ceiling are, however, unique and very beautiful, as is the altar screen and the canopied tombs.

Sidmouth's nicely ambiguous holiday slogan is 'Select Sidmouth'. Select it certainly is – one could almost say genteel; no amusements or cafés on The Esplanade, no funfairs in the back streets, no obvious signs of discotheques, little industry, and a population a large proportion of which is retired. It is also friendly,

*Budleigh Salterton beach, with a jumble of fishermen's gear, including a windlass to haul boats up the pebbly beach.*

decorative, charming, superbly situated, architecturally pleasing and, to cap it all, the views from its 500-foot high red sandstone cliffs are superb. Altogether a highly desirable place at which to spend a quiet holiday – but not perhaps with young children or teenagers.

Waves break on a beach of large pebbles when the tide is in, smaller pebbles and sand when it is out – a beach probably better suited for swimming from, rather than splashing about on. The Sidmouth Sailing Club has its headquarters at the eastern end of the beach and on race days several score dinghies are launched straight off the beach in a flurry of white sails and highly varnished hulls – quite a feat with any sort of sea running.

The half-dozen or so fishing boats are launched in the same dramatic way, but few fish are caught here nowadays. Yet in early

*Sidmouth beach, in wintry mood, with Chit Rocks and Peak Hill in the background.*

*One of Sidmouth's attractive streets, with every building different. Nothing distinguished here, but what a delightful mixture of styles in the small shops and houses.*

days this was quite a busy fishing and market town, only declining early in the nineteenth century. Like Torquay it benefited from the Napoleonic Wars when the upper and middle classes who would have travelled to the Continent looked instead for congenial surroundings in this country. Sidmouth's mild climate and glorious setting attracted them and they built 'cottages', some more like mansions in size and style. It is fortunate that this growth occurred at a time when architectural fashion was tasteful – if at times leaning towards the fanciful. Very little has been destroyed in the intervening years and the town is full of elegant little Regency and Georgian villas, with ironwork, arched windows and leaded lights, canopied verandas, and even bargeboards and thatch.

Some say that Sidmouth fossilized in an earlier century, but that is unkind. Even if there was an element of truth in it, why should a town not choose to linger in a more leisurely, tasteful age? The hotch-potch of styles is delightful and even the main shopping street has a line of shopfronts all completely different in style, yet matching in scale. Inside, many have the elegance and grace of a bygone era.

As well as its natural beauty, Sidmouth is well known for two people – Princess Victoria and Mrs Partington. In 1819 the Duke and Duchess of Kent (deep in debt, it is said, and with the Duke in ill health) travelled from Germany and settled in Sidmouth with their infant daughter, who was later to become Queen. They stayed at a cottage called Woolbrook Glen – now the Royal Glen Hotel – but within a short time the Duke died, leaving the infant princess as heir to the throne. This royal association naturally increased interest in the town and it continued to grow apace.

Mrs Partington was altogether a different type – a redoubtable character who lived at Chit Rock, in one of several cottages exposed to wind and tide. During one particularly bad storm her cottage was flooded and the good lady was seen with bucket and mop vigorously sweeping out the Atlantic Ocean. As fast as she cleared one corner the sea swept back in again and inevitably in the end she lost the valiant but unequal struggle. Perhaps she learned what Canute had proved much earlier – that there are some forces of nature that yield not to man nor beast! Her name is remembered because, at the time, her action in trying to stem the waves was likened in The Lords to the action of those trying to delay the progress of political reforms.

Branscombe village, a few miles up the coast, is a collection of tidy thatch and cob cottages, straggling untidily down a combe which leads to the sea, past a fine old pub and fourteenth-century church. The beach is pebble – large, small and medium-sized – with some of interesting colours. Undoubtedly, the best features are the cliff walks with superb views in both directions along the coast, from Sidmouth to Seaton, and beyond.

As you drive up the estuary of the River Axe, on the opposite bank you may see a tram keeping pace with you – yes, a brightly painted, open-top tram of the type so familiar in towns twenty to

*Branscombe village sprawls its way down a sheltered valley to this pebble beach at Branscombe Mouth. The whole area is owned by the National Trust and there are breathtaking views (in all senses) from the grassy slopes leading to Beer Head.*

thirty years ago. What is such a vehicle doing here, miles from the nearest large town and apparently setting off into the depths of the countryside, watched only by leisurely munching cows and the wild birds of the estuary? Well, it's a long story that began nearly thirty years ago when the late Claude Lane started building small trams to carry passengers at garden fêtes and seaside sites. By 1954 his company – Modern Electric Tramways Ltd – was operating full-scale trams at Eastbourne, and these proved extremely popular. Unfortunately, the tramway right-of-way was lost and he started looking for a new location for his fleet of six trams, one which would have a good catchment area for passengers and, most important, security of tenure.

*Open-top trams – not the sort of vehicle you expect to find trundling off into the countryside, let alone following the banks of the River Axe. But these are a tourist attraction with a difference, and they are also much appreciated by bird-watchers.*

Seaton seemed a good prospect with plenty of visitors and a roadbed ready to hand when B.R. closed their branch line from Seaton Junction to Seaton, early in 1966. He obtained an option on the three miles (and the blessing of the local authority), and eventually a building was erected to serve as a depot and new narrow-gauge track was laid. The first passenger-carrying car ran in the summer of 1970, using a specially constructed battery trailer which accompanied each tram. Inevitably there were problems, including near disaster when several new rails fractured under traffic and whole sections of track had to be replaced. Then a stroke of luck, for they managed to purchase a much tougher track recovered by the Sierra Leone Government Railway and returned to Britain as scrap. In 1971 Claude Lane died but, fortunately for the future of the project, Alan Gardner who had been with him for many years was able to take over as manager. Every year more passengers used the line and an extension around the perimeter of Warner's holiday camp to the council car park helped to swell the numbers.

Now a further extension is being built from Colyford to Colyton, again using rails from Sierra Leone, which incidentally were originally made in Britain many years ago. As well as being an unusual tourist attraction, the tram service is regularly used by local people and by others for another rather unusual purpose. Because the track runs alongside the Axe estuary, which is a natural sanctuary for wildfowl, it has become extremely popular with naturalists and bird-watchers. They use the trams – outside the hours of normal passenger services – as a novel form of mobile hide. Amongst the birds to be seen here are curlew, heron, oystercatcher, buzzard, teal, lapwing, woodpecker and many others – fifty-three varieties have been observed in a single day from the tramway.

In an age when governments reward mediocrity and conformity, and at best only tolerate initiative and enterprise, more power to the elbow of anyone with sufficient vision and expertise to provide what the public obviously wants and appreciates.

Although Seaton's beach is much the same as Sidmouth's and their superb cliffs are none too different, architecturally they are poles apart. Seaton developed late as a seaside resort and most of its buildings are late Victorian and Edwardian. If Sidmouth leans towards the staid and genteel, Seaton tends to favour the brash and modern, with a large holiday camp, souvenir shops and all the accoutrements of mass tourism. It makes no bones about being a family holiday resort in a beautiful setting.

Axmouth is worth more than the passing glance which is all one can normally spare when negotiating the sharp bend into the village, for this was once a busy and prosperous place. It sits snugly, but rather forlornly, $1\frac{1}{2}$ miles inland at the top of the Axe estuary. This huddle of cottages marks the point where a branch of the Fosse Way ended. When the Romans first arrived at this part of Dumnovia they found a well-established port and this they further developed for the export of wool and iron from the Mendips. In those days the estuary would have been much wider and deeper, probably half a mile or more across.

At some time in the Middle Ages a landslip on the Haven Cliff partially blocked the harbour entrance. Several attempts were made over the years to dig out the channel and, at one stage, a pier was built at which vessels of 100 tons could unload, but the harbour's days were numbered and eventually the shingle formed a huge bank around the fallen rock and sealed the entrance to all but small craft.

The port declined and houses and buildings were allowed to decay. Today the only reminder of its busy past is the Harbour Inn in Axmouth's main street. The present 'mouth of the Axe' is crossed by an old bridge said to be the first concrete bridge in Britain, and in the channel alongside is a haven for small boats. Five miles or so further along the coast lies the border of Dorset and the delights of Lyme Regis . . . but that's another story!

I always find canals fascinating places, whether disused and moribund, with the echoes of past glories, or alive with the throb of diesel-powered narrow boats, or the higher pitched note of the pleasure craft outboard. Almost unique in Britain, Tiverton Canal represents a waterway restored to use after a lapse of thirty years or so, but restricted to non-powered craft. The only sound is the gentle lapping of water against the hull of the *Tivertonian* as she moves at a gentle pace, and the occasional snort from Ben the Irish draught horse who shares with Captain – another sturdily independent character – the work of pulling the boat along this canal.

The *Tivertonian*, purpose-built in Yorkshire, has a steel hull 70 feet long and a beam of 10 feet, with traditional decorations on the cabin sides and characteristic tiller steering. She carries up to eighty passengers on public trips along the canal, quietly, without fuss, and incredibly smoothly. This is a fine example of the very little effort required to move waterborne craft (and, of course, cargoes) after the initial inertia has been overcome – quite literally

*The port of Axmouth has long since ceased to function and now lies one and a half miles inland up the silted estuary. Where river meets sea there is now a small haven for pleasure craft behind the sheltering pebble ridge.*

(Above) *Otterton, a village in the East Devon tradition of thatched roofs and ochre-washed walls. A stream, neatly channelled, runs down the main street.*

(Right) *Beer is famous for its stone and for smuggling. Its quarries provided material for Roman villas, cathedrals (including Exeter) and many a humble cottage. When quarrying ceased, smugglers moved in and found the underground galleries eminently suitable for their activities.*

one horse power (Ben in this instance) equals the pulling power of several lorries, or a double-decker bus.

The Grand Western Canal, of which this formed a part, had a chequered history. It was built during the 'canal mania' of the late eighteenth century when many fortunes were made, and lost, on navigable waterways. The original intention was to provide a route between the Bristol and English Channels, so that small ships could avoid the hazardous passage around Land's End. Other schemes had already failed, but in 1796 an Act was obtained to allow the Grand Western to run from Topsham, near Exeter, to Taunton – there connecting with the Rivers Tone and Parrett and thence to the sea via Bridgwater. There were to be branches to Cullompton, Tiverton and Wellington, a total of forty-six miles at an estimated cost of £166,724. They were no better at estimating costs in those days than now and this figure was to prove hopelessly wrong.

The plans were shelved, with costs rising due to inflation (and that also has a familiar ring), until 1809 – when the time seemed ripe to commence the work. Rennie resurveyed the route that had previously been chosen and the proprietors decided to start the canal in the middle – a disastrous choice as it turned out – in order to benefit from the carriage of limestone from Burlescombe quarries to Tiverton. This was never very profitable, whereas if they had started at the Taunton or Topsham ends there would have been an immediate trade in sea-borne coal.

Rennie also miscalculated; he decided to lower the summit level by sixteen feet to save the construction of locks, which are expensive to build and time-consuming in operation. Unfortunately, this involved a great deal of heavy and difficult cutting and embanking, with costs rocketing. When the eleven miles from Tiverton to Lowdwells were completed in 1812 they had cost £244,505, much more than the original estimate for the whole canal.

With money running out, the original ambitious scheme was

*Conversation piece on the eroded red cliffs of Ladram Bay.*

*This is Captain, the one horse power needed to pull the Tivertonian quietly and smoothly along the Tiverton Canal.*

*After a chequered history, Devon County Council took over the canal in 1971 and developed it as a linear country park. The boat trips are extremely popular, but the towpath is also a very pleasant place to walk.*

*There is little on the Tiverton Canal to disturb the peace of this family of swans, for power-craft are banned.*

abandoned and the proprietors accepted the suggestion of James Green, an Exeter engineer, that the canal should be completed from Lowdwells to Taunton on a reduced scale, in order to connect with the newly built Bridgwater and Taunton Canal, thus gaining access to a seaport. This section was eventually completed with seven vertical lifts and an inclined plane – advanced engineering for its day. Perhaps too advanced, for there were many mechanical failures and design problems.

Nevertheless, these were overcome and the section was opened in 1838. All seemed set fair for the proprietors to at last obtain a modest return on their capital. But it was not to be, for in 1844 along came the railway – the Bristol and Exeter, with a branch to Tiverton – and a long battle set in for freight. Competition caused both canal and railway companies to drastically reduce rates, but whereas the railways could set losses against profits elsewhere in the system, the canal company had only one source of income. Canal traffic was strangled and in 1854 the waterway was leased to the G.W.R., who eventually took it over completely. Inevitably maintenance was neglected and commercial traffic virtually ceased.

In 1971, Devon County Council very far sightedly bought the canal from the British Waterways Board, who in the intervening years had become responsible for it, and created a superb waterside park with a towpath that is a delight to walk upon. The old basin at Tiverton has been cleaned out and it is a pleasant place to sit and watch the sun dappling the water, or to see wildfowl diligently foraging amongst the canalside reeds in their eternal search for food.

By opening up and providing public access to this magnificent canal-side walk Devon County Council hope to divert a few of the visitors thundering down the M5 and relieve a little of the pressure on the more traditional and overcrowded holiday areas, such as Dartmoor and the coastal resorts.

Tiverton, a bustling, pleasant town, has other attractions too. Old Blundells School (a long rambling building erected in 1599) was founded by Peter Blundell, a wool merchant, during the town's wealthiest period. It is now in the care of the National Trust. Another property a few miles away to the north, and recently acquired by the National Trust, also has strong links with the history of the town. Knighthayes Court was designed by William Burges and built between 1869 and 1873 for John Heathcoat-Amory, the grandson of John Heathcoat, founder of the lace-making and knitting industry established in the town in 1816. This is a mellowed stone building with some fine interior woodwork and – as the estate agents would term it – well matured gardens, looking out over gently rolling countryside towards the town which provided the wealth for its building.

*Just above the tidal limit on the River Torridge lies the town of Great Torrington — above in all senses of the word, for the town sits astride a hilltop with a grinding climb up either side. This pattern of neat fields is seen from near the bowling green, once the site of a castle.*

# CHAPTER SEVEN

# NORTH DEVON

---

DEVON'S NORTH COAST is utterly different in character from the south coast. Here everything is on a grander scale – the sombre cliffs are higher, the beaches more extensive, and the long Atlantic swell beats against the rocky shore with devastating force. The same breakers, in gentler mood, provide the motive force for the premier sport of the coast – surf-riding.

Inland there are the neat patchwork fields around Great Torrington, the woods of the Torridge Valley, isolated hamlets and time-mellowed churches. Away on the foothills of Exmoor are the deep combes through which flow rapid streams – streams originating on the high moor beyond. On the hillsides, beech hedges turn a rich red in autumn. The county boundary follows a zigzag course through and around the slopes of Exmoor and it must be conceded that the lion's share of the moor lies in Somerset. Be that as it may, Devon has no cause for complaint, for she already has Dartmoor and, as a bonus, the glorious stretches of sand in Bideford Bay.

But let us look first at Hartland – town, quay and headland – merely a mile or so from the Cornish border. The town – it barely warrants the description nowadays – is a quiet place, mostly of one street leading to a small square. Yet in the past it was important, having been created a borough and allowed a market in the 1280s. Well off the beaten track, it failed to grow as did its near neighbours on the Taw and Torridge estuary and the market ceased in 1780, leaving it merely as the centre of a huge parish.

Hartland Quay, of which little remains today, was, surprisingly, quite an important port in the sixteenth century. Trade continued in coal, slate and limestone, etc. until well into the nineteenth century when the sea finally won and the small harbour was overwhelmed. Looking at the jagged fangs of rock and hostile sea it is difficult to imagine how boats ever manoeuvred in and out of here.

I last visited it on a gale-wracked day with ragged streamers of mist being torn to shreds against the high cliffs. Under such conditions it is an elemental, awesome place; one can almost feel the forces that created the stratified rocks. The cliffs are as though a giant hand had crumbled a piece of corrugated paper and then sliced clean through it with a knife. Smooth pebbles the size of wheelbarrows are thrown around like confetti on the beach. All is utter confusion and the cliffs tower menacingly above everything. At low tide there is a sandy beach, but it is certainly not the place to take the kids for a leisurely bathe.

Three miles away is Hartland Point. Even a hundred or so feet above the sea, the air tastes salty on the lips. In any wind, gulls are catapulted up and over the edge of the jagged rocks and swept past the lighthouse built in 1874 to give some protection to seafarers on this inhospitable coast. As the old saying has it,

> From Hartland Point
> To Padstow Light,
> A Watery Grave by
> Day or Night.

Before leaving the headland have a look at Hartland church (actually at Stoke). This is a splendid building with a fifteenth-century tower 128 feet high, a fine rood screen and an unusually high wagon roof giving a very spacious feeling.

Just up the coast is Clovelly, a tourist trap if ever there was one, but unself-consciously picturesque, charming and unique. In the summer you must expect to pay dearly for parking and to share its charms with hundreds of other visitors. In spite of all this Clovelly is a bright-and-shining sort of place of which the locals are justifiably proud. (It won a 'Britain in Bloom' award in 1975.) Even the abominable British habit of allowing litter to fall where it may appears to make little headway here. One feels that it must be whisked away almost before it touches the ground.

*It is difficult to believe that sailing craft once manoeuvred in and out of the tiny harbour at Hartland Quay. The jagged, stratified rocks are typical of this stretch of coast.*

The cobbled main street descends the steep hillside like a water-fall, with eddies into small courts and gardens, until it reaches the harbour far below. The colour-washed houses – mostly original and with few signs of 'tarting-up' – are everyone's idea of what a Devon village should look like. In fact, its only serious rival for the attention of photographers is Polperro on the South Cornish coast. Thousands of feet of film must be exposed here each year!

The Cary family really created Clovelly. Seven generations lived here between 1457 and 1724, but it was George Cary, a sheriff of Devon, who made the most impact – he built the massive stone harbour to provide protection for a small fishing fleet and

(Above) *A picture that sums up Clovelly's charms, cobbled steps — trodden by many thousands of feet each year — leading to white-washed cottages and a picturesque main street.*

(Left) *A visitor pauses to take a photograph of Clovelly Harbour, an event repeated many times each day in the summer. Who really could resist such a setting — old harbour wall, colourful boats, attractive pub and fine stone cottages?*

also many of the buildings. Donkeys were used to carry goods – and people – up and down the precipitous street. Their descendants have a much easier time today, taking children for short rides along a level path and occasionally carrying luggage, etc., to cottages in the village. From the harbour there is a Land Rover 'bus service' to carry the weary traveller back to the cliff-top car park via a less steep and better surfaced loop road.

Bideford and Barnstaple must be considered together, for not only are they just a few miles apart, their fortunes have always been linked. Both had a large share in trade to Ireland and America; Bideford probably cured more fish, but Barnstaple imported more wine and also dealt with a greater volume of inland trade.

In 1724, Defoe, returning up the north coast after having visited Land's End, reached the "Towns of Barnstable and Biddiford". He wrote:

> The first of these is the most ancient, the last the most flourishing. The harbour or river is in its entrance the same to both, and when they part, the Tower [Torridge] turning to the right, or south-west, and the Taw to the south-east, yet they seem to be both so safe, so easy in the channel, so equally good with respect to shipping, as equidistant from the sea, and so equally advantageous, that neither town complains of the bounty of the sea to them, or their situation by land; and yet of late years the town of Biddiford has flourished and the town of Barnstable declined.

He describes Bideford as "a clean and well-built town" with Bridgeland Street "as broad as the High Street of Excester" and well inhabited with considerable and wealthy merchants. He was intrigued by the several ships carrying rock salt from Liverpool and Warrington. This was dissolved in sea water to make 'salt upon salt' and used to cure herrings.

William Maton, writing in 1794 in his *Observations of the Western Counties of England*, also commented on the curing of fish from Newfoundland at Bideford, together with the landing of wool from Ireland. He too was impressed by the layout of the town:

> Bideford has to boast of a noble bridge, a most commodious wharf (situated in the heart of the town) and a body of water sufficient to

*Bideford Quay, tree-lined and quiet nowadays, but a hive of activity in the days of sailing craft. In the background, its bridge of twenty-four arches, all of different widths, with parts dating from 1699. Not far away is Victoria Park; around the base of the old grandstand are cannon said to have come from Armada galleons.*

bring up to it vessels of 500 tons, except at the ebb tide, when almost half the channel of the river is left dry. From standing quite on a declivity, this town is much cleaner than sea-ports usually are, and many of the streets are spacious and the abode of opulence.

Maton was primarily interested in the geology of the area but

he makes many other observations on the economy and architecture.

> Lime burning is a considerable article of trade at Bideford, one hundred tons of Welsh limestone being often burned in a day. And here is a large pottery, the clay of which is brought from Fremington, near Barnstable. A stratum of the fine reddish sort has been worked to the depth of more than twenty feet. It is procured at as easy a price as half-a-crown per ton.

From these old accounts a picture of the life of these ports emerges clearly and the activities of the work-people. Maton, in talking about the pottery, said: "I could not help shuddering at the effects that seemed likely to ensue from the practice (so prevalent in Devonshire) of keeping cyder in these vessels." He was very concerned about the lead added to the glaze and thought, quite rightly, that this would combine with the acid of the cider to cause lead poisoning, causing what was obviously an only too prevalent illness – 'Devonshire colic'. To make matters worse, it seems that lead was also deliberately added to the cider to impart sweetness and a softer flavour.

After these two accounts of Bideford it seems unbelievable that William Marshall's account – written just two years later – on *The Rural Economy of the West of England* should have this to say:

> The town of Bideford is remarkably forbidding. Meanly built houses (timber, brick, or mud, covered with bad slate or thatch) stuck against a steep hill. The streets, of course, are awkward; and most of them narrow. In the vacant spaces between the streets, immense piles of furze faggots rise, in the shape of houses, and make the houses themselves appear more like hovels than they really are.

Well, the town could not have changed that much in so short a time, so we must assume that this jaundiced view was caused by a less than perfect meal at the inn!

If these worthy gentlemen retraced their steps today, what would

*The statue of Charles Kingsley on Bideford Quay.*

they find? The streets are as broad, the bridge as noble, but the quays are deserted and many of the activities that they mentioned have long since ceased. Like so many other places in Devon, Bideford lives very much off the tourist trade nowadays.

Barnstaple claims to be an older town than Bideford, in fact it claims to be one of the oldest boroughs in England, with a charter dating from 930. It had a mint around the same time and issued its own coins. The town grew at the highest navigable reach of the river, close to the point where it was also most easily fordable. In the fourteenth century it was the third town in Devon, surpassed in importance only by Exeter and Plymouth. It had a considerable woollen industry for several centuries, but by the eighteenth century this had ceased and, ironically, Barnstaple had become the principal port for the import of Irish wool and yarn. This was then transported overland to the small towns of east and mid-Devon where it was turned into serge.

Defoe found it "a large, spacious, well-built town", whilst Maton remarks: "Few towns have a more neat and comfortable appearance than Barnstaple. It contains at least four thousand inhabitants. There are prosperous manufactories of waistcoats, silk stockings etc. and a variety of articles are exported." Even Marshall was moderately pleased – perhaps he had lunched better that day. "The town of Barnstaple is respectable. The streets are wider and better laid out, than those of old towns generally are. Many of the houses are substantially built of brick." However, he had to have one last dig: "But the covering here is of the same mean-looking slate as that which is in use at Bedeford."

Today, Barnstaple possesses an unenviably complex one-way traffic system which converges on the funnel-mouth of its sixteen-arch bridge, much altered from the original built in the fifteenth century. Its shopping streets have character and would certainly benefit from the removal of through traffic. Worth seeing is the Pannier Market and Butchers Row, a street of small open-fronted shops, many still used by butchers. Also Queen Anne's Walk, where ship-owners and merchants once conducted their business.

On the south side of the river is Barnstaple's latest and proudest possession – a lavish and expensive Leisure Complex, catering for

Barnstaple's shopping centre has much character, but is usually jam-packed with cars negotiating its fiendish one-way traffic system. Not far away is the site of the former Great Quay from which, a plaque tells us, there sailed in 1588 'five of the six ships from North Devon which joined Sir Francis Drake's fleet at Plymouth, and helped to defeat the Spanish Armada'. They were The Dudley, The God Save Her, The Tiger, The John of Barnstaple, and The Unicorn, or The Prudence.

(Overleaf) *Probably in Victorian times, Lynmouth became known as 'The English Switzerland', from the tree-covered 'mountains' that surround the tiny harbour – in the same way as any town in Europe with a canal or river acquires the tag of 'The Venice of . . . .'. Lynmouth suffered grievously in the floods of 1952, but lost none of its character in the re-building. Mars Hill, in the background, is one of the most attractive rows of thatched cottages in the county.*

every sport under the sun. Or to be more accurate, not under the sun, for all activities are indoors and it is designed to entice summer visitors from the beaches on dull days and to cater for local people from all over North Devon.

On the quayside at Bideford stands a statue of Charles Kingsley with pen in one hand and book in the other. Really it would be more appropriate at Westward Ho! (or Northam) for it was his novel that made the area popular and created the resort. On second thought, No! – for he was not overfond of the idea of development and wrote to a friend, "How goes the Northam Burrows scheme for spoiling that beautiful place with hotels and villas? I suppose it must be, but you will frighten away all the sea pies and defile the Pebble Ridge with chicken bones and sandwich scraps."

He was right, of course, and now for good measure there is prize bingo, Tyrolean beer gardens, and row upon row of chalets. The pebble bar, however, is still magnificent and there is a sandy beach at low tide. Sea pies, incidentally, were a sailors' dish made of salt-meat, vegetables and dumplings, all baked together.

Kingsley was born at Holne in South Devon, son of a vicar. While he was still young the family moved to Clovelly and the memories and stories of North Devon life gained during these formative years were to stand him in good stead in later years. They next moved to London, but in 1854 Kingsley returned to Bideford to write his most famous book – a stirring tale, full of life and fire and compassion. Just the adventure story to stir the blood of youngsters of his time. He wrote many other books including *The Water Babies*, but none fired the public imagination in the same way as this story of naval exploits against the might of Spain. It was here too that he wrote his well-known poem 'The Three Fishers' about Bideford Bar, a sandbank at the mouth of the estuary.

Between Bideford and Westward Ho! lies Appledore, a village

*The Tome Stone, at Barnstaple, which was used by merchants to settle accounts. Money changed hands across the stone, in front of witnesses, and this then constituted a legal transaction. It is much the same as the four bronze 'nails' outside Bristol's Corn Exchange, from which came the phrase 'paying on the nail'.*

that has changed hardly at all over the years. It supplied several ships for Sir Francis Drake's fleet and if they sailed back today I doubt if they would notice anything very different. Just a score or so years ago, I can remember sailing schooners tied up at the quayside and looking thoroughly in keeping with the place.

It is a village of seafarers' houses – sea captains of old in their bow-windowed residences, the crews in more humble dwellings. A place to stroll through slowly exploring the odd corners. For example there is a One End Street, the first house of which is One, One End Street. Could there, I wonder, be a T'Other End Street somewhere? Just off the quay is a Trinity House buoy store full of brightly painted monsters of the deep, no doubt in for overhaul, rather as one services a car. Ten thousand wave service, perhaps?

Tall ships used to land tobacco and cod, from Virginia and Newfoundland. Local fishermen have always landed their catches here – and still do. Their small boats tear off down the river with each tide, out to the mouth of the estuary where the fish are. When I visited there recently, on the sandy mud bottom (or perhaps it should be muddy sand) were sitting a motley collection of craft – several fishing boats, two glass-fibre cruisers, a clutch of sailing dinghies (the wind playing a lively tune on their rigging), the pilot boat, and an ancient motorized barge, named rather optimistically *U.F.O.*

Ship-building has always been important to Appledore, but one thing is certain: if Drake's sailors returned today they would be overwhelmed by the large covered yard of Appledore Shipbuilders Ltd, just upriver from the village. Here they turn out an amazing variety of quality boats from tugs to small tankers, patrol boats to dredgers.

From the Taw and Torridge estuary as far as Morte Point, 'North Devon's Golden Coast' becomes fact as well as advertising slogan. The golden sands stretch away for mile upon mile backed by the sand-dunes of Braunton Burrows (all 1,000 acres) which serve birds as a nature reserve and people as a suntrap on windy days. At Saunton a rocky headland breaks the rhythm, but not for long, for just over the headland is Croyde. As well as the beach there is an attractive village here of thatch and white-washed cottages.

Baggy Point is National Trust owned and from here we get our first view of the five-mile-long beach at Woolacombe, probably the most popular of all the North Devon beaches. Popular though it may be, there is room for all, and sitting on the flower-covered dunes it is still possible to find solitude. Listening to the distant sound of breaking waves and running the soft sand through one's fingers, William Blake's words come to mind:

> To see the world in a grain of sand,
> And a heaven in a wild flower

The razor-edged slate cliffs of Morte Point have claimed many a victim – five ships in one winter alone, in 1852. For this reason a lighthouse was built in 1879 at Bull Point, not far away. Much of the area is owned by the National Trust, Morte Point having been

*Saunton Sands are part of 'North Devon's Golden Coast'. Three miles of glorious sand, backed by the 1,000 or so acres of Braunton Burrows. Part of the dunes is a nature reserve.*

given by Miss R. Chichester in 1909 in memory of her parents and the remainder bought in 1970 from 'Enterprise Neptune' funds.

Ilfracombe is advertised as the 'Friendly Holiday Resort and Golden Coast Tour Centre', which is an awful mouthful, but also a very fair summing-up. It is one of my favourite resorts, for it never tries to be what it isn't. There is no veneer of expensive five-star hotels, or concrete filing-cabinet blocks of flats; neither, at the other end of the scale, have pin-tables, candy floss and bingo been allowed to dominate the seafront. Between these extremes it caters admirably for family holidays.

In character it is completely different from other Devon resorts – an up-hill down-dale sort of place, straggling over several hills, with its main street and shopping centre 100 feet or so above the harbour. To gain an idea of the layout, climb the gorse-covered slopes of Hillsborough Hill which dominates one end of the town. There below is the narrow entrance to the harbour with precipitous cliffs to landward – the entrance needs to be narrow to keep out the surprisingly steep seas from the Bristol Channel. Just inside is the jetty at which Campbell's White Funnel Line steamers tie up, on their trips from Swansea, Penarth, Porlock, and Lundy.

Beyond again is the inner harbour, always bustling with sea-going life, but never more so than when a gale sends dozens of craft scuttling for shelter in one of the very few really safe havens on this treacherous coast. A glorious jumble of craft, from the *Lundy Gannet* (the supply ship for the island) to the smallest of fibre-glass runabouts, with an ever-dwindling number of fishing boats tied up against the harbour wall. It dries out at low water leaving sand at one end soft enough for children to dig sand castles, whilst lower down there is sandy mud sufficiently firm to allow vehicles to be driven on to service the boats.

Crowning the narrow peninsula at the entrance to the harbour is Lantern Hill and on top St Nicholas's Chapel – an ancient building

*There is a surprisingly Mediterranean-like air about Ilfracombe Harbour. Perhaps it's the blueness of the water, the sandy beach, the colour-washed houses – or maybe the palm trees. This is always a busy place bustling with a mixture of pleasure and working craft.*

and seamark that has been much altered over the years. A fine collection of colour-washed houses jostle for position around the harbourside, with restaurants and souvenir and pottery shops well represented.

To entertain its visitors Ilfracombe provides a small golf course on the lower slopes of Hillsborough, a go-kart track tucked discreetly away in a hollow, and just beyond an indoor swimming-pool of very respectable proportions. For sea-bathing there are a number of beaches, mostly in small coves, several of the most popular being reached through a tunnel in the cliffs.

Do make the effort to climb the cliffs of Torrs Park for the magnificent panorama from the top; the town is laid out below and there are views along the coast in each direction. Go there of an evening and you will see sunsets to delight a thousand shepherds (or sailors), with the lights of the Welsh coast shimmering away in the distance like a host of marine glow-worms. The locals claim that the lights of eight Bristol Channel lighthouses and buoys are visible from here.

Even Ilfracombe's most ardent admirer would not claim that, in general, her architecture was distinguished – 'homely' might be a better word. However, within striking distance are two country houses – Chambercombe and Arlington – entirely different in character and both well worth seeing. Chambercombe Estate occupies a valley only a mile or so from the town centre and could well be in danger of eventual engulfment by caravan sites and industrial building. The manor house dates basically from the eleventh century, but it came into the possession of Sir Henry Champernon, Lord of the Manor of Ilfracombe, in 1162. It remained in the hands of the same family until the fifteenth century, eventually passing to the Duke of Suffolk. At some time after this it fell from its high estate and became a farmhouse.

*Chambercombe Manor dates basically from the eleventh century. Inside the mellowed stone building there are low ceilings, massive oak beams and some fine old furniture, including a bed in which Lady Jane Grey is reputed to have slept. A pleasant place to visit and to take tea in the old courtyard.*

It is a small, compact house of mellowed stone, nestling in a well-wooded hollow with lakes and herb garden. Inside, there are low ceilings, huge oak beams (probably made by shipwrights, for they are like ship's timbers), thick walls and a lime ash floor which resembles polished granite, so smooth has it become with the passage of time and countless feet. There are several pieces of fine furniture – including a beautifully carved four-poster bed in what was at one time Lady Jane Grey's room – and Cromwellian suits of armour.

Like all really old houses it has its ghost story – one based on fact too. It seems that in 1765 a tenant farmer was repairing the roof when he noticed the outline of an old window which did not correspond with any room inside. Being curious he pulled down an inner wall which he thought merely separated the house into two parts. Beyond he found a small room partly hidden within the thickness of the walls. Inside were the remains of a bedstead and resting on this the skeleton of a woman.

The legend goes that this was of a titled lady rescued from a shipwreck at Hele. She was alive when rescued, but her face was disfigured and she later died in the house. The occupants kept her jewellery and sealed off the room so that the theft would not be discovered. Perhaps it is stretching credibility rather far, but the story has a sequel. The woman was later identified as the daughter of the then tenant who had married a rich man in Ireland and was returning to visit her parents. Without being recognized she had come home and died in her father's arms. Rather a sad story. Her ghostly figure is said to appear from time to time in the room where she died, or a cold presence is felt in the corridor.

Arlington Court is altogether grander, but also much more modern. The house – now owned by the National Trust – is surrounded by a park in which graze a flock of Jacob's sheep and a herd of Shetland ponies, friendly creatures much photographed by visitors. The Court was designed by Thomas Lee of Barnstaple in 1820–3. Outside it is plain, almost ugly, relieved only by a semi-circular Greek Doric porch. Inside it is a very different story: all rooms open on to a central hall with fine sweeping staircase. Doors lead to a saloon furnished with French and English furniture; beyond there is a dining-room mellow with mahogany and silver.

There are more than 400 years of history in these old box-pews in Molland church. Whatever other purpose they may have served, these shoulder-high 'compartments' would have had the very practical effect of shielding the occupants from cold draughts — very comforting to body and soul — in the days before central heating.

The house was built for the Chichester family who had owned the estate from the fourteenth century and it is full of family mementoes. Miss Rosalie Chichester who lived here from 1908 until her death in 1949 was an ardent collector of pewter, porcelain, shells, paintings, snuff boxes, ships models, *objets d'art* – in fact, almost anything small and intriguing, and her character can be felt throughout the whole place. It is almost an intrusion to walk into some of the rooms, so vivid is her presence.

The stable block close by contains a fine collection of horse-drawn vehicles and harness, and the gardens with their rhododendron walks and lake make a pleasant place to idle away an hour or so.

On the night of 15 August 1952 there was a torrential downpour on the high hills of Exmoor and within hours the moorland streams had become raging torrents. The East and West Lyn were no exceptions, and straddling the narrow rocky valley where they flowed to the sea was Lynmouth. With virtually no warning the peat-stained waters swept through the village – and others further up the valley – with devastating force. Thirty-one people lost their lives and ninety-three homes were destroyed.

The village was rebuilt, together with a replica of the little red-topped tower on the end of the pier originally built by General Rawdon as a copy of a Rhenish structure. Scars have healed and the river now flows in disciplined order down the valley between concrete banks, across the pebble beach and into the sea. The harbour is a pleasant haven on a rocky coast, for pleasure craft, a few fishing boats and the various boats taking visitors on 'trips round the bay'.

At some time – probably in Victorian days – Lynmouth acquired the tag of 'The English Switzerland'. The phrase has a ring of the Great Western Railway's *Holiday Haunts,* a publication dear to the hearts of older travellers, but it must be admitted that the branch line from Barnstaple to Lynmouth was owned by the *Southern* Railway Company. Be that as it may, the name stuck, which is a pity really for the area is quite capable of standing on its own without comparison with 'foreign parts'. The scenery is superb, with cliffs 800 feet or more in height rising sheer from the sea. Inland there are wooded ravines almost too steep to support

*Sheep were around long before cars! The view a motorist so often sees of farm life on the byways of the county A fluid milling mass of four-legged uncertainty – the despair of any sheep-dog. However, given a little patience and tolerance, the muddle soon sorts itself out.*

213

*Malmsmead and Badgworthy Water lie right on the border between Devon and Somerset. This is fine Exmoor walking country with wooded valleys and rolling hills.*

the trees that cover their sides. Do walk the 1½ miles or so up the valley to Waters Meet where the East Lyn and a tributary, the Hoaroak Water, come together in a dramatic and beautiful setting. The whole of this area is now owned by the National Trust.

Like many another of Devon's resorts, Lynmouth became popular during the Napoleonic Wars. In later years visitors found that it had one major disadvantage – there was a steep hill separating Lynton at the top, where many of the hotels were situated, from Lynmouth at the bottom with its harbour and beaches. The hill was too steep for motor cars and although there was a donkey service to carry visitors, this was expensive – and hard on the donkeys! Everyone pondered on the problem and eventually a Mr

Bob Jones came up with a novel device for a cliff railway, and the publisher George Newnes, who often visited the village and loved the area, provided the financial backing for the construction.

The railway, unique in Britain, was opened in 1890. Built at an angle of about 30 degrees in a cleft in the cliff-face, it rises for a vertical height of 450 feet or so. Two cars with water tanks in their bases work rather like kitchen scales; as one tank is filled (700 gallons at a time) the car becomes heavier and moves off down the track, at the same time pulling up the other lighter car. Each carries twenty passengers and the whole railway is still very popular with visitors.

Not far from Lynton is the magnificent Valley of Rocks – and Lee Bay (for good measure there are two in North Devon) and Woody Bay. Inland don't miss Malmsmead and Brendon. Then there's Foreland Point – oh, the list goes on and on. There is so much more of Devon, but here on the steep cliffs within sight of the Somerset border we must stop.

*Generally, North Devon's coastline is rugged, dramatic and wild, but there are exceptions. Woody Bay is in a more gentle style, with hanging woods almost to the water's edge, backed by fields and gorse-covered cliffs. A toll road winds through the woods, with superb views where there are gaps.*

In the end it is the small things one remembers of a journey, like kaleidoscope pictures — the sea-faded pastel shades of fishermen's nets, the spring yellow of primrose-lined hedgerows, the cloying flavour of thick clotted cream, the intolerant mewing of gulls, a squabble of sparrows scattering dust on a village green, the steely grey slabs of gaunt cliffs, the quiet satisfaction of all (onlookers included) as the last bale of hay is humped up on to the trailer as daylight fades. Devon is indeed a beautiful county and that beauty is so worth preserving.

*The last bale of hay is gathered in on a North Devon farm. A reminder of the importance that farming plays in the county's economy.*

# END PIECE

As for the future, who knows? I believe it was Banquo in Shakespeare's *Macbeth* who said, "Look into the seeds of time, and say which grain will grow and which will not." The one single 'grain' most likely to shape Devon's future character is the motor car – once beloved by all, now the *bête noire* of all planners.

Perhaps we are all over-reacting to the four-wheeled invasion and under-estimating its benefits! Has the pendulum swung too far? Small towns appear to have quite happily absorbed this monster with which we all have such a love–hate relationship – and are doing very-nicely-thank-you in terms of trade, mostly by building cheap (or free) car parks close to their shops. Only the large cities appear to have insoluble problems with inadequate and expensive parking, coupled with inadequate and expensive public transport.

Will motorists eventually desert the city centres and head for the out-of-town hyper-markets? The trend is already there. These markets overcome parking problems and place shopping facilities where they are needed, but just look at the valuable farm land they occupy. Can anyone justify further removal of trade from city centres, with all that it leads to – less rated property, decaying buildings, fewer amenities, higher prices, and so on. Heaven forbid that our cities should eventually become merely architectural museums!

It is easy to pose the questions and to state the problems. Only a committee composed of Solomon, Old Moore and the Three Wise Men, and chaired by the Archangel Gabriel, could hope to find satisfactory answers. I wish the planners well, they will certainly need to put an additional polish on their crystal balls, dampen their seaweed, and still keep their fingers crossed. Plans fall like autumn leaves – transportation studies, structure plans and the like – but in the end it is the people living in the county who will decide how they want to live and work.

Next to tourism, farming is Devon's main industry – and I trust my farming friends will forgive me for placing them in that order, but in recent years one has outstripped the other in terms of revenue, if not in importance. For as long as I can remember, farmers have complained of having a thin time, whether through government interference (or indifference), lack of support (or too many controls), cheap imports, middlemen's profits, high taxation, estate duty, too much rain (or too little rain) – all as they took delivery of their new Rovers, Jaguars and Volvos.

Now the days of crying wolf are over; farmers have taken a thorough bashing in the past few years. Land values rocketed – and then plummeted. Paper millionaires became paper paupers almost overnight. Beef prices sunk so low and feed stuff costs rose so steeply that stock was abandoned outside Devon's abattoirs. At the time of writing some sanity has returned and farmers will receive more for their produce, but the 1976 drought drastically cut milk production. All in all, my friends assure me that a farmer's lot is still not a happy one.

No doubt they will continue to grumble – and to switch from beef to milk to arable, depending on current political fashion, but let us hope that one day a government (of any persuasion) will realize that people *must* be fed and that farming is one of the most important industries in the country.

Whatever changes take place, the essential qualities of Devon will remain for a very long time yet – the winding country lanes between deep hedgerows, the neat pocket-handkerchief-sized fields, the solitude of Dartmoor, the ceaseless rumble of waves pounding on our cliffs and beaches – always provided that we do not take it all too much for granted!

If I may end with the words of the old adage, "Today is the tomorrow you worried about yesterday – and all is well." True, but perhaps all is well because someone in the past cared enough to want to preserve it all.

# INDEX

*Illustration page numbers are in bold figures*

**Abbot's Way**, 94
Abercrombie, Sir Patrick, 33
Adam, Robert, 44
A La Ronde, **163**
Alfred, King, 133
Alvington, 60
Amicia, Countess of Devon, 82
Anglo-Saxon Cronicle, 20
Appledore, 38, 202
—— Shipbuilders, 204
*Ark Royal*, 167
Arlington Court, 209, 210, 212
Armada, Spanish, 23, 109, 135, 167
Ashburton, 74, 81
Aveton Gifford, 52, **54**
Avon Dam, 80
Axmouth, 177, 178, **179**

**Baggy Point**, 205
Badgworthy Water, **214**
Baldwin, Norman Lord, 134
Bantham, 53
Barnstaple, 194, 198, **199**, 202, 203
—— Charter, 198
—— Leisure Complex, 198, 202
——, Pannier Market, 198
——, Queen Anne's Walk, 198
—— Trade, 194
Battle of Hastings, 104, 134
Bedford, Dukes of, 90
Beer, **180**
*Bellerophon*, 110
Bellever, 93
Berry Head, 109

Bideford, 194, **195, 196**
—— Bridge, **195**
—— Pottery, 197
—— Trade, 194, 197
Bigbury-on-Sea, 52, 53, 54, **55**
Black Down Hills, 161
Blackpool Sands, **68**
Blake, William, 205
Blundell, Peter, 187
Blundell's School (old), 187
Bolt Head, 56, **57**
Bolt Tail, 56
Bowerman's Nose, 101, 102, **103**
Branscombe, 174, **175**
Braunton Burrows, 204, **205**
Brendon, 215
Bridgwater and Taunton Canal, 186
Bristol and Exeter Railway, 139, 186
British Rail, 156
Brittany Ferries, 16, 31, **32**, 42
Brixham, 28, 48, 109, 116, 122, 123, **124, 125**
Bronescombe, Bishop, 148
Brunel, Atmospheric Railway, 154
Brutus, 126
Buckfast Abbey, 94
Buckfastleigh Station, 118
Buckland Abbey, **76**, 82, 94
Buckland-in-the-Moor, 97, **98**
Budleigh Salterton, 170, **171**
Burgh Island, 52, **55**
Burlescombe Quarries, 183
Burrator Reservoir, **79**, 80, 81, 83
Butterfield, 49
Bytton, Bishop, 148

**Cadiz**, 23
Caerwisc, 133
Calstock, 42
Campbell's Steamers, 206
Cape of Good Hope, 23
Carter, Ken, 149
Cary, George, 191
Castle Drogo, 102
Cecil, Lord, 169
Celtic Tribes, 20
Chagford, 97
Chambercombe Manor, **208**, 209
Champernon, Sir Henry, 209
Champernowne, family, 130
Charles I, King, 26
Charles II, King, 26, 149
Cherry Brook, 93
Chichester, Sir Francis, 24
———, Miss Rosalie, 206, 212
Childe's Tomb, 94, **95**, 96
China Clay, 77, **78**
Cistercian Monks, 82
Civil War, 26, 56
Clapper Bridges, **93**
Clovelly, 190, 191, **192**, **193**, 194, 202
Cockington, **108**, 114, 115
Colyford, 177
Colyton, 177
*Compton Castle*, 62
Cookworthy, William, 60
Courtenay, family, 104
Crediton, 134
Cromwell, 149
Croyde, 204

**Danish Pirates**, 133, 147, 162
Dartington, 128,
——— Hall, 128, **131**
——— School, 130
——— Trust, 130
———, Twelve Apostles, 131
Dartmeet, 93
Dartmoor, 33, 77
——— China Clay Pits, **78**
——— Leats, **83**, **84**
——— National Park Committee, 77, 106
——— Pony Express, 106
——— Preservation Association, 77, 80
——— Reservoirs, 79, 80

———, Service use of, 77, 105
———, Walking, 105
Dartmouth, 24, 63, 67, 68, **70**, 71, **72/73**
169
———, Bayards Cove, 74
——— Castle, **70**, 71
———, Royal Naval College, 67
———, St. Petrox Church, 71
——— Steamers, 74
Dart Valley Railway, **118**, 119
Darwin, 'Origin of Species', 114
Dawlish, 153, 154, **155**
——— Lawn Gardens, 153,
——— Strand, 154
Dawlish Warren, 156, 157
*Defiance*, 157
Defoe, Daniel, 19, 67, 138, 194, 198
Devon,
——— Farming, **216**, 217, 218
——— Future, 217, 218
——— Tourism, 16, 217
Devon County Council, 48, 77, 187
Dodbrooke, 60
Domesday Survey, 20
Drake, Sir Francis, 19, 21, 76, 82, 90, 135,
137, 204
———, Circumnavigation by, 23
———, Game of Bowls, 23
———, Leat built by, 28
Drewe, Julius, 102
Dumnovia, 177

**Earl of Essex**, 167
Earls of Devon, 138
East Budleigh, 168
Eddystone Reef, 30
El Dorado, 169
Elizabeth, Queen, 21, 23, 28, 130, 164,
166, 167, 169
Elmhirst, Dorothy and Leonard, 130
Enterprise Neptune, 206
Exeter, 42, 133, 161
——— Canal, 138, **139**
——— Cathedral, 147, **148**, 149, **150**, **151**,
**152**, **153**, 170
——— Charters, 134
———, Countess Weir, 138
———, Exanceaster, 133
——— Guildhall, **132**, 147

—— High Street, **143**
—— Maritime Museum, **140**, 141
——, Mol's Coffee House, 135, **137**
——, Princesshay, 145
——, Rougemont Castle, **134**
——, Rougemont Gardens, 133, 145
——, St. Mary Steps, **145**, **146**
——, Ship Inn, **136**, 137
——, Southernhay, 133
——, Stepcote Hill, **145**
—— Underground Passages, 145, 146
—— University, 153
Exmoor, 161
Exmouth, 48, 161, 162, 163, 164
—— Docks, 162
—— Marine Drive, 164, **165**

**Falcon**, 165
FitzGilbert, Baldwin, 104
Fosse Way, 177
Fox Tor, 96
France, 68, 71, 110
French Line, 31
Frobisher, 135

**Gardner, Alan** 177
Gilbert, Sir Humphrey, 21, 135, 165
*Golden Hind*, **22**, 23
Good Hope, Cape of, 23
Goodrington, **112**
Grand Western Canal, 183
Grandison, Bishop, 170
Great Torrington, **188**, 189
Great Western Railway, 187, 212
—— Tenders, 31
Green, James, 186
Grenville, Sir Richard, 82
Grey, Lady Jane, 209, 210
Grimspound, 94
Guilebridge, 96
*Gypsy Moth III*, 24
Gytha, 134

**Hallsands**, **62**, 63
Harold, 134
Hartland, 189, 190, **191**
—— Point, 189
—— Quay, 189, 190
—— Town, 189

Hawke, Admiral, 110
Hawkins, John, 21, 135, 167
Hawley, John, 71
Hayes Barton, 165, **166**
Haytor, **100**
—— Tramway, 99, 100, **101**
Heathcoat, John, 187
Heathcoat-Amory, John, 187
Hemerdon Bank, 15
Henry II, King, 71
Henry III, King, 138
Henry IV, King, 68
Henry VIII, King, 90
High Willhays, 105
Holland, John, 128
Hope Cove, 56
Hope, Inner, 56
Hope, Outer, 56
Howe, Admiral, 110

**Ilfracombe**, 206, **207**
——, Entertainments in, 209
—— Harbour, 206, **207**
——, Hillsborough Hill, 206, 209
——, Lantern Hill, 206
——, Torrs Park, 209
International Sailing Craft Association, 140
Isabella, Countess of Devon, 138
Isca Dumnoniorum, 133
Island Cruising Club, 58
Ivybridge, 15, 81

**James I, King**, 169
James II, King, 28
Jones, Bob, 215

**Kathleen and May**, **18**, 38
Keats, 159
Kent, Duke and Duchess of, 174
Kent's Cavern, 113
Keymis, Laurance, 169
Kingsley, Charles, **196**, 202
Kingsbridge, 53, 60, **61**
—— Estuary, 47, 48, **61**
——, Fore Street, 60
——, St. Edmund's Church, 61
Kingswear, 74
Kitley House, 49

Knighthayes Court, 187

M5 Motorway, 16, 42, 47, 139

**Ladram Bay, 182**
Lane, Claude, 175, 176
Lee Bay, 215
Lee Moor, 78
Lee, Thomas, 210
Lelend, 122, 137
Leofric, Bishop, 134, 147
Lich Way, 96
Littleham Cove, 164
Local Government Reorganization, 20, 42
Lustleigh, 97
Lutyens, Sir Edwin, 102
Lydford, 96
Lynmouth, **200**, 212, 214
Lynton, 214, 215

**Madre de Dios**, 169
Maidencombe, 116
Magellan Strait, 23
Malmsmead, 214, 215
Manaton, 97, 101
Maritime Museum (Exeter), **140**
Maritime Trust, 38
Marshall, William, 197, 198
——, 'Rural Economy of the West of England' by, 197
Martin, Sarah, 49
Mary Tavy, 85
Maton, William, 194, 195, 196
——, 'Observations of the Western Counties of England' by, 194
*Mayflower*, 24, 25, 26, 74
——Memorial, **25**
Meavy, 85, **87**
Meldon, Reservoir, 80
Millais, Painting of Raleigh, 165
Mill Bay, **58**
Millbrook Steamboat Company, 42
Modbury, 51, **53**
Modern Electric Tramways Ltd, 175, **176**
Molland, **211**
Monmouth, Duke of, 27
Moretonhampstead, 96, 97
Morte Point, 205
Morwellham Centre, 90
Mothecombe, 49, **50**, 51
Mother Hubbards Cottage, 49

**Napoleon**, 110
Napoleonic Wars, 28, 109, 111, 173
National Trust, 43, 52, 58, 76, 82, 92, 102, 175, 187, 205, 210, 214
Nelson, Admiral, 110
Ness, The, **158**, 159
Newcomin, Thomas, 74
Newnes, George, 215
Newman, Mary, 21
Newton Ferrers, 42, **46**, 49
Nombre de Dies Bay, 23
*Normandie*, 31
Normans, 20
Northam Burrows, 202
North Bovey, 97, **99**
North Devon's Golden Coast, 48, 204
North Hessary Tor, 85
Northcott Theatre, 153
*Northumberland,* 110
Noss Mayo, **46**, 49
*Nostra Senora Del Rosario*, 109

**Oddicombe**, 116
Okehampton, 102, 104
——Castle, 104
Oldway House, 116, **117**
'Onedin Line', 74, 141
Orcombe Rocks, 164, **165**
Otterton, **180**
Ottery St. Mary, 170

**Paignton, 111**, 112, **113**, 116, 164
——Festival Theatre, 113, 164
——Harbour, **111**
Parker, John and Lady Catherine, 44
Parminster, Misses, 163
Parson and the Clerk, 157, 158
Partington, Mrs, 174
Paton-Watson, James, 33
*Pelican*, 23
Pengelly, William, 114
Pettyjohn, Miss, 63
Phillip, King of Spain, 21, 23
Pilgrim Fathers, 19, **24**, 38, 74
Piper, John, 38
Plymbridge, **45**

Plymouth, 19, 141, 142
—— Barbican, 18, **24**, 38
—— Breakwater, 31
——, Blitz on, 33
——, Cattewater, 28, 31, 38
——, Charles Church, 26, **35**
—— Charter, 20, 28
—— Citadel, 26, **27**
—— Civic Centre, 33, 38, 43
——, Devil's Point, 28
——, Devonport, 29
—— District Council, 20, 42
—— Dock, 28
—— Dockyard, 29, 30, 39
——, Drake Circus, **37**
——, Drake's Island (St. Nicholas Island), 21, 38, 39
——, Elizabethan House, 38
——, Freedom Fields Park, 26
——, Grand Design, 39
—— Guildhall, 34, 38, 39, **40**
——, Hamoaze, 28
—— Hoe, 26, **29**, 30, 39, 42, **43**, 93
——, Island House, **24**, 38
——, Mayflower Memorial, **25**, 38
——, Millbay Docks, 31, 39
——, Plan for Plymouth, 33
—— Royal Parade, 33, **34**, **40**, **41**
——, St. Andrew's Church, 26, 34, 39
——, Smeaton's Tower, **27**, **29**, 30
—— Sound, 19, 26, **27**, 39, 169
——, Sutton Harbour, 20, 31, 38
——, Union Street, 32, 39
'Point-in-View', 164
Postbridge, **93**
Prayer Book Rebellion, 135
Priors of Plympton, 20
Princetown, 85, **86**

**Quivil, Bishop**, 148

**Raleigh, Sir Walter**, 21, 28, 110, 164, 165, 166, 167, 168, 169, 170
——, Expedition to Guiana by, 169
—— Execution of, 170
—— Knighted, 167
Rennie, John, 183
Reynolds, Sir Joshua, 44
Richard Coeur De Lion, 71

Richard II, King, 71
Ringmoor Down, **81**
Rivers,
—— Avon, 48, 52, 53
—— Dart, 47, 48, 93, 126
—— Erme, 15, 48, 49
—— Exe, 138, 161
—— Lyn, East and West, 212, 214
—— Plym, **44**
—— Tamar, 42, 90
—— Tavy, **90**, 96
—— Taw, 194, 204
—— Teign, 102
—— Torridge, 188, 189, 194, 204
—— Yealm, 42, **46**, 47, 48
Roborough Down, **83**, 106, **107**
Rodney, Admiral, 110
*Roebuck*, 110
Romans, 19, 133
Roscoff Ferry, 31
Rose, Sir Alec, 140
Royal Navy, 31
Royal Western Yacht Club, 42
Rudyard, 30

**St. Canute**, **140**, 141
St. Malo, 31
St. Vincent, Admiral, 110
Salcombe, 53, 56, **58**, **59**
Saltram House, 42, 43, **44**
Saunton, 17, 204, **205**
Saxons, 161, 177
Seaton, 161, 177
—— Tramway, 175, **176**, 177
Shaldon, 159
Shaugh Prior, 80
Sheeps Tor, **79**, **81**
Shovel, Admiral, 110
Sidmouth, 170, **172**, **173**, 174
——, Chit Rock, 172, 174
—— Sailing Club, 171
——, Woolbrook Glen, 174
Singer, Paris, 116
Slapton, **62**, 63, **64**, **65**, 66
——, Ley Nature Reserve, 63, **65**
—— Obelisk, 65, **66**
Smeaton, John, 30
Smeaton's Tower, **27**, **29**, 30
Smith, Margaret, 34

Soar Mill Cove, 56
South Devon Railway Company, 112, 154
South Devon Riviera, 48
South Hams, 47
—— District Council, 47
South West Peninsula Footpath, 17
Southern Railway Company, 212
Spain, 21, 23, 164
Spanish Barn, 110
*Speedwell*, 26, 74
Spitchwick, 81
Stapledon, Bishop, 149
Starcross, 156
Start Point, 62
Stokenham, 67, **69**
Stover Canal, 99
Stukely, Sir Lewis, 170
Sudtone, 20
Suffolk, Duke of, 209
Sutton Prior, 20
Sutton Ralf, 20
Sutton Valletort, 20
Sweyn of Denmark, 134
Swincombe, 80

**Tamar Bridge**, 39
Tavistock, 81, 89, 90, **91**
——, Benedictine Abbey, 89, 94, 96
—— Canal, 90
Taylor Coleridge, Samuel, 170
Teignmouth, 109, **158**, 159, 164
Templer, George, 99, 159
Throckmorton, Elizabeth, 167
Thurlestone, 56
Tiverton, 161, **183, 184, 185**, 186, 187
—— Canal, 178, **183, 184, 185**, 186
——, Old Blundell's School, 187
——, *Tivertonian*, 178, **184, 185**
Topsham, 138, **160**, 161, 162
Tor Royal Estate, 86
Torbay, 109–125
—— Aircraft Museum, 119, 122, **123**
——, County Borough of, 113
Torcross, 63, **64**, 65
Torpoint Ferry, 39
Torquay, 111, 112, 113, **114, 115**
——, Abbey Sands, **120, 121**
——, Anstey's Cove, 116
—— Inner Harbour, **114**, 116

—— Marine Drive, 115
——, Rock Walk, **114**, 115
——, Thatcher Rock, **115**
——, Torre Abbey and Gardens, 110, **120, 121**
*Tory*, 38
Totnes, 71, 118, 126, **127**, 128, **129**
——, Brutus Stone, 126
——, Butterwalk, **127**, 128
—— Castle, 126
——, East Gate, **129**
—— Guildhall, 128
—— Quays, 126, 127
——, Ramparts Walk, 128
Trew, John, 138
Tyrwhitt, Thomas, 86

**Uncle Tom Cobleigh**, 97
United States Army Authorities, 65, 67

**Valley of Rocks**, 215
Victoria, Princess, 174
Vixana, 87, 88
Vixen Tor, 87, **88**

**Walla Brook**, 96
Warelwast, Bishop William, 147
*Warspite*, 30
Waters Meet, 214
Westward Ho!, 202
Wheal Betsy, **92**
Wheal Crowndale, 90
Widecombe-in-the-Moor, 97, 98
William I, King, 20
William III, King, 28
William of Orange, 28, 110, **125**
William the Conqueror, 134
Winstanley, Henry, 30
Woody Bay, **215**
Wonwell, 51
Woolacombe, 17, 205

**Yealmpton**, 49
——, Mother Hubbard's Cottage, 49
——, St. Bartholomew's Church, 49
Yelverton, 81

**Zeuse**, 157